RENDEZVOUS BY SUBMARINE

Rendezvous By Submarine

The Story of Charles Parsons and the Guerrilla-Soldiers in the Philippines

By

Travis Ingham

Rendezvous By Submarine: The Story of Charles Parsons and the Guerrilla-Soldiers in the Philippines by Travis Ingham.

Published by The Bowsprit Press, Los Angeles.

FIRST PRINTING 2018.

ISBN-13: 978-1726302135.

ISBN-10: 172630213X.

CONTENTS

FOREWORD BY CARLOS P. ROMULO

In prewar Manila, before the Japanese made a place of hell out of our city that was the playground and paradise of the Far East, I often saw Chick Parsons through a chukka of polo. He was considered one of the best players in the Islands. To watch the sun-bronzed Chick at play, as if his entire soul were tied into the game, was to observe an American who had in every way fitted into our easy Philippine manner of living.

Chick was one of us in Manila before the war. I saw Chick Parsons in Manila again, after MacArthur's return, after the liberation of the Philippines. It was the biggest moment in both our lives. There was very little left of the Manila we had known; nevertheless, we who in Malacanan Palace that day heard President Sergio Osmena offer his praise and thanks to the American hero, Commander Parsons, realized that Chick had come home.

The American and Philippine flags were flying together over the old palace, and it was the lean, hard-bitten Chick who had helped put them back there.

Because Chick Parsons went in ahead of the rest of us. He led the invasion by a year. For the year preceding the landing of our Allied forces on Leyte Beach, Chick Parsons had been a powerful name that must not be spoken but that was always in the thoughts of eighteen million Filipinos and of the members of General Douglas MacArthur's staff.

It was MacArthur who sent Chick Parsons back into the Philippines.

When, from the captive Philippines, a few faint radio signals came in (proof that Filipino resistance was not dead), General MacArthur selected Chick Parsons to go by submarine into the Jap-infested Islands and help the fighting Filipinos drum up coordinated resistance. He left on this strange and dangerous mission, and the friendly, playful Chick ceased to exist. "Commander X" took his place in history and in the minds of those who knew of this amazing and daring attempt to co-ordinate and equip an army within a captive country. Chick's American friends, many of them, thought of him as dead. The Japanese hunted him in vain through the Islands and finally announced his death over Radio Tokyo.

But eighteen million Filipinos knew Chick Parsons was alive and in the Islands. He had brought them MacArthur's renewed pledge: "I shall return!" This was Chick's message to Garcia, and its delivery is one of the strangest epics in fighting history. That slogan moved a nation to resist and held eighteen million suffering people in sublime faith to a single man: MacArthur.

How Chick got through with his message, and how he was aided and protected by the Filipinos, and how he in turn thinks and feels about them, is ably told in this book in Chick's own laconic fashion, as he has told it to Travis Ingham. His tributes to Filipino loyalty touch my heart.

For the Filipino as you see him today stands in rags in his ruined country. He was a proud man before the war. He took pride in his American education, his American clothing, his American standards of living. The ragged, fighting Filipino who met the Allied soldiers on the beaches of Leyte and Luzon was the image of beggary, but there was, and is, no beggary in his heart. He is still the proudest man in the world.

He is proud because he fought for America and democracy and freedom and because with all his limited power he helped beat the way to Allied victory, and in his heart is the sound of drums.

Chick Parsons helped set the beat of those drums.

As MacArthur's coordinator of Filipino resistance, Commander Parsons knows the bloody story of that fight from within as no other American can ever know it.

Every word written here is the truth, as told by a great scout, a good soldier, and a heroic American who knows and loves the Filipinos and the Philippines. It is the story from the inside of the Filipinos' life-and-death struggle to stand by America.

Let me in turn speak of Chick Parsons from the Filipinos' point of view.

I know how they looked upon him, the emissary of MacArthur, the lone, brave American making his brave way over our mountain trails, always a few steps ahead of the brutal Japanese. I know how they feared for him, guarded him, fought for him—even died for him.

Their love for him was in their faces when they surrounded him on Leyte after the fight was won there, and again in Manila when the exciting game was over and our land was set free. They crowded around him, in trust and admiration, for a great coordinator had returned to the city that again was ours.

On that day of triumph in our shattered Manila, I saw Chick Parsons come into his own. He had risked his life to come back. His contribution to Americans and Filipinos alike was beyond estimate, for we shall never be able to compute how many lives were saved by the careful planning of the invasion, from the inside, by information supplied and assistance rendered by the guerrilla army.

That day in Manila I realized that men like Chick Parsons and the Filipinos who fought with him, and cities like Manila, never die. Our paradise in the Far East will rise again and in it Chick Parsons will be living with that grand family of his, and once again I shall drop over to the Polo Club to see him through a chukka of polo. As long as Manila stands, as long as Filipinos remain proud and free, Chick Parsons will remain "one of ours."

V-E Day
Peace Conference
San Francisco
May 8, 1945

PROLOGUE

All my trips to the Philippine Islands, for the purpose of contacting and supplying guerrilla-soldiers, have been of a routine and uninteresting nature.

MIDNIGHT OFF MINDANAO. MARCH 1943.

A periscope, like the hooded head of a sea serpent, broke the rippled surface of a vast bay and made leisurely reconnaissance. Finding nothing for apparent alarm on the nearby waters or in the dark distant mass that was the shore, the submarine surfaced. The sea slipped silently from its back, a hatch opened, and five figures crawled out on deck.

There was the hiss of oxygen escaping from metal into rubber as a small boat was inflated. Two men, naked to the waist, took their places at the paddles. These were Moros and the land beyond belonged to them, once. Instinctively, they fingered the long bolos at their belts and their eyes, disquieted, sought each other in the gloom.

The third man to step into the boat was an American naval officer, but there was nothing to indicate this now.

Only slightly taller than the Moros, broad-shouldered, sturdy, he wore a pair of nondescript shorts, a bleached and tattered khaki shirt. Around his neck hung a pair of canvas sandals. His head and feet were bare.

Chick Parsons, Lieutenant Commander, USNR, was going home too.

The two officers left on deck handed down a waterproof knapsack. They saw the familiar flash of Parsons' teeth as he grinned, saw him raise his left hand, the thumb and forefinger making a circle-symbol of the American serviceman for approval and luck. Then they climbed back into the submarine, which sank silently to the bottom, there to wait.

Nothing now on the surface of the bay except a swirl of white foam and the doughnut-shaped boat moving in toward the faraway crescent of the lagoon.

The winds of morning began to stir and little whitecaps slapped the sides of the awkward raft. The outward tide gained strength and the paddlers grunted softly as they dipped deeper against the currents. There was no moon but almost imperceptibly it became lighter as the rubber boat inched toward a break in the reef.

The tropic dawn was hurrying. Already sentinel shapes of palm trees were visible and the sand blurred white along the shore.

They let us off too far out, thought Parsons and unconsciously sank his fingers into the yielding sides of the boat. "Pas, pas," he whispered to the Moros. "Faster!"

The paddlers dug deeper and presently thrust the boat through the green passage between coral heads and into the lagoon, into quieter waters. This was better. Perhaps they might yet make the shore and fade into the countryside without detection—cheating the eye of dawn and the enemy, should he be about.

Thus the American thought and breathed easier when, without warning, the darkness still clinging to the brush beneath the palms flamed yellow. Bullets whined over the rubber boat, struck the water nearby, and sighed off into the distance.

"Japanese!" whispered the Moros, their paddles freezing in mid-air, the soft hair on their necks lifting with the breath of eternity in passage. Their eyes huge with fear, they turned to their leader, for they were jungle fighters caught in an alien element.

To turn and run at this point, Parsons knew, was possible death. Sure admission of guilt and failure of their project. There was only one thing to do.

"Go on," he ordered. "It is too late to turn."

The Moros murmured in their own dialect. Falteringly their paddles sought the water again. The little boat shoved on . . . into another volley. But scattered this time. Not so sure. Some of the men behind the rifles showed doubt, anyway. They could be seen now, slipping from tree to tree as though in conference. They could not yet be identified.

If they were friendly Filipinos and guerrillas, good—providing the more trigger-happy did not mow them down before shore could be reached and explanations given. If they were Japanese a story would have to be invented—and a thousand rushed through Parsons' mind as the boat proceeded steadily on its course. None of them seemed any good.

If the Japanese suspected that the three men in the boat were belligerents, if they realized that the broad-shouldered man in the tattered shirt was the same party who had left Manila under peculiar circumstances several months before . . .

A year—actually fifteen minutes—seemed to pass from the moment of the first volley until the rubber boat slewed up in the wash of the beach. Still inventing and discarding possible stories, Parsons stepped out and made his way up the sand toward the menacing underbrush. He carried no arms, no ammunition, nothing.

From behind a coconut tree a figure with rifle at alert stepped out. He wore the peaked cap of a Japanese infantryman. His ragged shirt was of similar origin. The shorts were neutral with age. But—and here the spirits of the officer soared—his feet were bare. The Japanese do not go bare-footed.

"Salud, amigo," cried Chick Parsons.

"Quien es usted?" growled the guerrilla, raising his rifle a bit.

"A messenger from General Douglas MacArthur," was the reply. "I bring you greetings from the Big Chief and supplies from his headquarters in Australia." He pointed toward the boat.

Other figures rose from the brush, accompanied their leader to the boat. Watched silently as Chick opened his waterproof bag. Stared, without comprehension, at the American cigarettes he offered them.

Then they let out a shout—and the palm trees and the holes beneath them sprang into life. Ragged little men, garbed in bizarre bits of American and Japanese uniforms, rushed down the beach. They swarmed over Lieutenant Commander Parsons, snatching at the cigarettes and gum, smothering him with the enthusiasm of their embraces. Women and children followed close on the heels of the fighting men. The sick and aged left their fires in the nearby village and hobbled eagerly to the beach.

The sun came up out of Mindanao Sea.

The tough, hard-bitten guerrilla-soldiers took the cigarettes and squatted in the sand with tears running down their cheeks. It was not just the thought of having in their hands something which had not been tasted or enjoyed in more than two years that moved them. This particular item had come from outside, from Allied sources, from the headquarters of General MacArthur and the United States of America. It had been carried aboard submarine through minefields and depth bombs. It had been delivered in person by a representative of the United States Navy.

All this meant to the guerrilla-soldier just one thing. It meant that his long wait in the wilderness had not been in vain: that his prayers and hopes were to be answered.

It was the first tangible sign of General MacArthur's long-anticipated return to the Philippines. The first bit of 'Aid'—as the people had come to know the word—which had been received since his departure. It was without shame that the guerrilla-soldiers squatted in the sand, and smoked, and let their tears flow freely.

PART I

THE MOVEMENT

CHAPTER I

I AM NOT A COLORFUL FIGURE AND I WISH to be kept out of the story of the guerrilla movement as much as possible. Whatever success I may have had in accomplishing my mission has been due entirely to the fact that my knowledge of the language and the people has made it possible for me to "blend in" with the country and so pass unnoticed by the enemy.

To understand the background of the guerrilla movement in the Philippine Islands—its growth from a mere idea at the time of Corregidor's fall to a trained army of jungle fighters, perfectly coordinated with American forces at invasion time—it is necessary to understand the background of the men who have been responsible for this movement.

It is impossible to have a free movement without freemen. Love of freedom is the major link between the lawyers, doctors, tradesmen, farmers, and unsurrendered soldiers who became the personnel and backbone of this movement in the Islands.

But love of freedom alone is not enough.

To be successful a free movement must be encouraged by outside sources. It must be supplied with arms and ammunition. It must be synchronized by a communications system. It must be directed and disciplined by capable and trusted leaders. It must operate according to a plan.

Among free movements in history the story of the guerrillas of the Philippines is unique. In no other similar movement have all these functions been assumed and discharged, with success, by a single man.

A man who first brought out definite proof to General MacArthur that a free movement was not only possible but underway in the Islands; who formed an Army-Navy team to supply this movement with the necessary equipment and ship it by submarine. A man who went into the Islands himself, time and again, under the most hazardous of circumstances to set up proper leadership, assure the safe delivery of arms, ammunition, and medicines, establish coast-watcher and radio stations, and evacuate valuable American and Allied personnel from the clutches of the Japanese. A man who withal worked in such modesty and secrecy that only once—when the Japanese announced with cries of "Banzai!" that he was dead and buried—did his name make the papers, but who is still carrying on in the hills and jungles, behind the dwindling lines of the Japs.

Parsons, known to the Army and Navy as Chick of the Spy Squadron, Spyron.

It's a long jump from Shelbyville, Tennessee, where Charles Parsons was born in 1902, to the Philippine Islands and a major role in a global war. Americans make those jumps, however, because they are . . . Americans. Chick's two uncles on his mother's side had gone out to the Philippines to seek their fortunes and their letters fired the boy's youthful imagination, appealed to his love of adventure. In the Chattanooga schools he took courses in stenography and shorthand and acquired a working knowledge of Spanish. After a year or two of practice as a court stenographer Chick made his way to the West Coast via side door Pullman, signed on a freighter as a member of the crew, and presently found himself alone, broke and nineteen years old—on the beach at Manila.

He stayed there only long enough to get his bearings. His knowledge of stenography plus Spanish enabled him to qualify for the job of secretary to Leonard Wood, then head of the Wood-Forbes Investigating Committee. For the next three years, Chick accompanied Wood on his yacht, the Apo, to all parts of the Islands. He got to know the terrain, meet the people, learn the language and the customs.

He began to blend in with the country.

A postgraduate course in commerce at the University of the Philippines, plus an ever-growing fluency in the local idiom, enabled Chick to land his next job, with the Philippine Telephone and Telegraph Company. In 1927 he had a chance to go to Zamboanga in Mindanao with the Meyer Muzzall Company, financed and operated by then Mayor Rolph of San Francisco, later governor of the state of California. The business of this company was the exporting of logs and lumber to the United States. As a buyer Chick traveled up and down the coast of Mindanao, second largest island in the group, until he knew it like a book; he hadn't the slightest idea this knowledge would many times save his life in years shortly to come.

Chick Parsons' approach to the Philippines was unlike that of the usual young American adventurer. From the first he had no desire simply to spend a few lucrative years in the Islands and return home to spend the money. This was home and, to emphasize the fact beyond further possibility of doubt, while he was in Zamboanga Chick married Katraushka Jurika, daughter of a naturalized Czechoslovakian, Stephen Jurika, and Blanche Walker, of Oxnard, California.

Katsy—it is pronounced "Cotsy"—was only fifteen. Chick about thirty. That never has made any difference.

"There I was in my pigtails and bloomers," Katsy explained, "and here came Chick with his big grin, and that was all there was to it."

Stephen Jurika had come to the Islands as a soldier in 1898. He had married there, and all of his children including Tommy—now a major and Chick's right-hand man in Spyron—were born in the Philippines. In marrying into this family, Chick married into the country and placed the final stamp on his blending-in process. He loved and understood the people—a sentiment which was mutually reciprocated. He spoke their language, figuratively and literally. He was completely and irrevocably identified with the Islands.

Moving on up into Manila, Katsy busied herself with family matters which presently involved three small male editions of their father, who meanwhile began a manager association with a string of businesses with which, if they exist, he is still connected.

Two young Americans had organized the North American Trading and Importing Company for the salvaging of alcohol from a hitherto waste product of sugar refining—molasses. This appeared to Chick to have possibilities and he became manager of this young industry, and also of the La Insula Cigar and Cigarette Factory, one of the largest tobacco interests in the Islands and owned by Spanish royalty. Presently he added the managership of the Luzon Stevedoring Company to his list and with it the operation of a fleet of tugboats, a series of chrome and manganese mines, and other activities with which this company was involved.

The last-named company and job are responsible for the title Chick likes best—that of boss stevedore. He also claims to be the only polo-playing stevedore in the world and with the Elizalde brothers founded the Los Tamaros Club in Manila to assure proper high-goal competition.

For a boy brought up in landlocked Tennessee, the sea has always been amazingly familiar to Chick Parsons. In 1929 he joined the Naval Reserve of the Islands and as a lieutenant, junior grade, took active duty with the fleet whenever possible.

By the fall of 1941 the Parsons fortunes had prospered to the point where Chick thought he might retire and devote his declining years—from the age of thirty-nine on—to polo, Katsy, young Michael, Peter, and Patrick Parsons, and the good life. Fate and a couple of Jap flattops had other plans in store for him, however.

Manila is a full day ahead of Pearl Harbor. On the night of December 8, Chick was awakened by a brother reserve officer, informed that the entire personnel and equipment of the Luzon Stevedoring Company had been taken into the United States Navy, was brought before Admiral Hart and sworn into active duty as a lieutenant, senior grade.

Davao, chief city of Mindanao, had been bombed by the Japanese. War had come to the Islands.

This, briefly, was Chick's schooling for destiny. What of the men he was soon to lead, direct, and supply—the guerrillas?

During the months that Bataan was being besieged, the southern and central islands of the Philippines were relatively free from enemy interest or effort. During this period USAFFE (United States Armed Forces in the Far East) was increasing its manpower by recruiting as many eligible Filipinos as possible from the areas near which the various divisions under General William Fletcher Sharp, commander of Mindanao and the Visayas, were stationed.

These men were all volunteers, ranging in age from seventeen to twenty-four, able-bodied, eager. They were brought into the service, armed, and trained to the fullest extent possible in a limited time. For, while it was quite apparent to the commanders in the south and central islands that Bataan and Corregidor could not hold out indefinitely, nevertheless a fight to the finish, and beyond, was anticipated.

Plans had been made to continue a guerrilla type of warfare should the enemy forces landing in these areas prove too strong to be met in open battle. Caches of food, ammunition, and other materiel were placed in the mountains and General Sharp intended to utilize to the highest extent the natural ability of the Filipino soldier for guerrilla-style warfare.

When General Wainwright surrendered Corregidor on May 7 he was forced to order all USAFFE forces in the central and southern islands to yield to the enemy. This the top officers in these areas at first flatly refused to do. They argued that their commands were intact, morale high, equipment built up to a point where they felt well and fully justified in resisting the enemy to the death. They also indicated that if necessary, at the same time, mountain warfare could be carried on indefinitely and to the definite embarrassment of the enemy.

As a man, General Sharp doubtless felt much sympathy with the stand of his subordinates. As an officer, he had to obey orders.

Furthermore, General Sharp had no reason to believe that a successful battle could be carried on indefinitely against the Japanese. Inevitably, without reinforcements from the United States, he must have felt, the USAFFE forces would fall. Therefore in order to avoid the massacre of thousands of prisoners held at Corregidor and possible retaliation by the Japanese against the prisoners of Bataan—with the sole benefit of a few weeks' continued resistance—General Sharp capitulated. On the twenty-ninth of May he surrendered all USAFFE forces in the central and southern sections.

The fall of the Islands was now complete.

At this surrender there were in the various districts, as has been indicated, large numbers of partially trained recruits. These men did not feel as though they should surrender and cast in their lot with the American soldiers, now that resistance was at an end. They were, after all, civilians—clerks, businessmen, farmers. It was much easier for them to put away their rifles and ammunition and return to civil life than to take a chance on surrendering with the Yanks.

Apparently the USAFFE officers did not make much effort to persuade these men to surrender. As a matter of fact it is presumed that the commanders, in turning in to the Japanese their rosters of personnel, purposely omitted the names of men who lived in the territory and had been but newly recruited. These volunteers therefore returned to their homes, buried their arms, and settled down at their old occupations to wait for the coming of the 'Aid' and the return of MacArthur.

During the months of June, July, and August 1942, the Japanese infiltrated the territory of the south by establishing garrisons in the larger cities and outposts in the little towns. To a very limited extent they endeavored to patrol the farm and mountainous country.

This occupation was accomplished without opposition and by a relatively limited number of troops. The Japanese found it more convenient and comfortable to group themselves in the larger cities and towns where, due to the terroristic methods of their secret police, they were easily able to submit the people to their will and whims. In other words, the same process which had been begun in Manila immediately upon occupation now extended itself to the south and central sections.

Outside of the cities and larger towns the rest of the country was very lightly held. In many cases garrisons consisted of not over one hundred men, outposts of only half a dozen. This left the major portion of the country without any police control whatever as the Philippine Constabulary, originally numbering seven or eight thousand men, had been demobilized with the invasion.

Here was a golden opportunity for the lawless element among the people to cash in, and they were not long in taking advantage of the situation. Bands of underworld characters and opportunists began to drift out into the hinterland, utilizing one excuse or another for preying upon the innocent farmers. With a show of force and arms they proceeded to take clothing, food, money, and equipment from their victims.

This went on for a month or so without resistance. At some point—and it seems to have been spontaneous all over the lower islands—the unsurrendered soldiers who had reclaimed their civilian pursuits decided the time had come to take a hand. By digging up their arms and banding together, they felt, they could police their home territory against these brigands. They therefore proceeded to organize on a small scale for war against the immediate peril of banditry.

While, as has been said, the Filipinos never stopped fighting, there was at first no thought of concerted action against the Japanese—who in most cases were miles away and rarely, if ever, seen. These were vigilantes pure and simple, operating as did law-abiding citizens in our old West. By day farmers and merchants, at night they would meet on the outskirts of town for whatever policing was necessary. It was only a small jump for several small town or rural groups to pool their arms and reserves for mutual protection of larger area.

The lawless element, being unorganized, was quickly dissuaded from its depredating ways, but vigilance remained. Furthermore these boys were now imbued with a lodge spirit. They felt a pride and power in organization.

Hence, instead of relaxing and laying down their arms, thereby permitting a possible recurrence of violence, they reinforced themselves and kept together.

The Japanese were not unaware of the potentialities for troublemaking of large numbers of armed citizens abroad in the land. Hence, they showered the unsurrendered soldiers with all manner of inducements to persuade them to come in and give up their arms. Freedom, good jobs, and the assurance that nothing would happen to them were among the persuasive promises dropped on the unsurrendered soldiers from the air and over the radio. A few of the more timid souls did surrender. The majority, however, mindful of the ever-present threat of banditry, preferred to hold onto their arms and take their chances.

With General Sharp's surrender a substantial number of officers, both Filipino and American, had of their own volition gone to the hills. These officers as a rule were professional soldiers who had been in the service some time and who were not in a position to return to civil life, as were the newly recruited soldiers. Furthermore, they considered themselves deserters—a belief in which they had been encouraged by the controlled broadcasts of their former commanders, General Wainwright and General Sharp.

These men took a very poor view of Japanese cajolery. They had learned what happened to the prisoners on Bataan and Corregidor and knew that Jap promises were not worth the paper they were printed on. Inevitably, therefore, as time went on, officers came in contact with vigilante groups and were asked to lead them. In many cases they were the same officers who had trained the young volunteers. The latter had come to respect the wisdom of these men, to recognize and obey their silver and gold bars. Even though these bars were now tarnished and the uniforms tattered and bizarre, it made no difference.

It was only natural that these captains and lieutenants with their new-found commands should contact each other and try to persuade their friends in the hills to head up leaderless groups. The military system asserted itself and district commands were set up, controlling numbers of smaller groups.

The occupation of Luzon had been accomplished so swiftly and completely that such a process was not possible to the extent that it was in the southern and central districts. But all over the lightly occupied sections it was taking place.

While the handwriting on the wall was not immediately apparent to the young Filipinos so organized, the background for a true guerrilla movement was there, and some of the necessary equipment and all of the spirit of free men stirring in chains.

Early in October 1942 the powerful Mackay Radio Monitoring Station at San Francisco bent its sensitive ear toward the Philippines. Weak but persistent signals were coming from a short-wave radio station in the hills of Panay, sixth largest of the Islands.

"Calling America . . ." the faraway voice repeated over and over, and gave its message in plain language—the message that freedom still lived in the hills, nourished by a band of men who were armed and organized and who realized now as never before the beautiful ways of democracy which they had lost. These men under Macario Peralta, a major of the Philippine Army, had already gone out against the enemy and would again so long as ammunition and life remained.

Would America listen this time, would she send the aid she had so often promised to her little people?

"Calling America . . ."

These messages were relayed to Washington, to the office of G-2 in charge of Colonel J. K. Evans. Were they authentic? the Intelligence Section wondered. Was there a real guerrilla movement at work in the Philippines? Or was this just another Japanese trick to decoy supplies and men to disaster?

"Over in Navy Intelligence is an officer who has just come back from the Philippines," the colonel was told. "He might have an angle on this."

The colonel looked amazed.

"Did you just say a United States naval officer just got out of the Islands?"

"Sure. Guy named Parsons. Escaped with his wife and three kids, one of 'em a baby!"

"How in heaven's name did he manage that?"

"Claims he hitchhiked—most of the way."

The colonel sent for Parsons.

CHAPTER II

THE CIRCUMSTANCES OF MY DEPARTURE FROM MANILA were, to say the least, rather peculiar.

When Charles Parsons, his wife, and three little boys walked down the gangplank of the Gripsholm in New York on August 29, 1942, he found that he had been officially listed by the Navy for the past nine months as MIA. This was only partly true. Chick Parsons had certainly been active enough during this period, but recently promoted Lieutenant Commander Parsons, USNR, had vanished completely in a bonfire of Navy uniforms in the compound of a large white house in Manila on New Year's Day.

Buttons of brass do not yield to flame as easily as suntans, however. Chick and Katsy therefore gathered up the blackened insignia and drove to an island in the Pasig River. The gloom that hung over the city of Manila on that day of hopelessness was physical as well as spiritual, the river a sea of flame as the oil tanks yielded their contents to the elements instead of the Japanese.

All during December 1941, Parsons had directed the pumping of that precious oil into American submarines that crept into the docks under cover of darkness, took on fuel and torpedoes, and nosed out through the minefields to try to stem the deluge of Japanese invasion forces.

Working with the port director's office, Chick had helped clean out the vast warehouses, taking the contents to Corregidor and Bataan, returning with the heroic dead.

The Japanese landed at Batangas on the twenty-ninth of December and Manila was doomed.

On New Year's Eve, Chick set forth on a macabre and terrible celebration: to welcome 1942 to Manila with torch and demolition bomb. Katsy insisted on going with him. They made a strange sight as they walked from dock to dock, Chick in his soiled Navy uniform, his wife in high-heeled slippers and a shimmery evening gown. At each pier, Chick gave an order to a group of shadowy figures, and in the wake of this command, huge warehouses full of peacetime commerce of the Seven Seas roared into sound and fury.

At length only one dock remained. Here were gathered brother officers, newspapermen, and friends who were taking the last boat to Corregidor and, as they thought, safety. Almost tearfully the members of this group implored the Parsons to join them. It was suicidal, or worse, they pointed out, to stay in Manila—as though Chick had not heard of Hong Kong, as though he did not have two women—his wife and mother-in-law, not to mention three small children—to worry about.

Lieutenant Commander Parsons had done his duty. Now, Chick Parsons felt, his place was with his family, for better or worse.

The boat shoved off. The little men, lurking in the darkness, rose from their haunches and moved forward.

"Ahora, Capitan?" they whispered. "Now?"

"Ahora, amigos," Chick replied softly, his eyes large with the enigma of the night and the immediate future.

Presently, alone on the veranda of the Army and Navy Club, Chick and Katsy watched the final pier go up in flames. They had burned their last bridge. Silently they drank a toast to dying Manila, the city that symbolized everything Chick had come to love in his twenty years in the Islands. He put a coin in the jukebox. Against a backdrop of flame the New Year came in while they slowly circled the floor in a waltz—the man in his grimy uniform, the girl in her oil-soaked evening gown.

Then they gathered Chick's uniforms from his locker and went home.

In the dawn of the terrible new day, Chick and Katsy stood on the banks of the Pasig and consigned his emblems of rank and loyalty to the swift current. Turning toward home and the inevitability of a concentration camp, they came upon an odd sight. A couple of blocks from the Japanese Club they met hundreds of civilians dressed in white, lining the streets and waving Japanese flags. These were the native-born Japanese, the sympathizers, the chicken-hearted, and the opportunists.

Martial music was coming from the direction of Avenue Taft, farther on, and at a street junction two civilian sentries wearing Rising Sun brassards jumped on the running board.

"We are commandeering this car to drive to Paranaque," they said.

"What for?" Chick inquired.

"To meet the Honorable General Homa, who is coming in with the victory parade to show the unenlightened the glory and power of the Emperor."

Chick had not expected the victory parade until the next day. One glance at the throngs on the sidewalks convinced him that he was practically leading it. He looked the sentry calmly in the eye.

"This city may belong to the Japanese tomorrow," he said quietly. "Today it is still American."

With that—and a whispered instruction to Katsy—they shoved the sentries off the running boards and the car darted away, followed by shouts and a few harmless bullets.

The next morning they awakened to a city silent as a tomb, a sky for once completely empty of bombers. Before their gate a Jap sentry walked his post and on the iron grill was a white seal which said: "Property of the Imperial Japanese Government."

Wearily the Parsons family gathered their belongings for the ordered move to the concentration camp at Santo Tomas. Just as the Japanese truck drove up, Chick's dark face lightened and he snapped his fingers.

"Hell," he said, "they can't do this to us. I'm the Panamanian consul."

"Honorary consul for Panama," Katsy corrected him.

"What's the difference," Chick inquired with his wide grin, "to the Nips?"

At the time of Pearl Harbor a number of Danish ships in the harbor had been seized and registered under the flag of Panama. The President of that country, on this information, had dispatched a career man to take over. Pending his arrival, Chick had been requested to act as "honorary consul" and the seals of office and identification papers so to empower him were now in his possession.

Quickly Chick dug out this evidence and sent Katsy and her mother, both of whom had resided briefly in Japan, down to the gate to talk to the Japanese. They were brandishing these credentials in front of the eyes of the puzzled sentries when little Mike, Chick's eight-year-old and eldest son, burst from the house.

"You can't take us to any old concentration camp," he shouted in Spanish. "My daddy's an officer in the Navy."

Fortunately, the sentries did not understand Spanish. Mrs. Jurika snaked Mike up into the house and explained to him the facts of life in Manila at the moment. Katsy reiterated her claim, while Chick, who was so sunburned that he could easily have passed for a Central American at that moment, appeared with a Panamanian flag which he had found among the kids' toys. This he proceeded to run up on the flagpole in the middle of the compound. The guards bowed. The truck departed. Within an hour Japanese consular officials appeared, hissing like radiators and begging to see the honorable credentials of the honorable consul from Panama. Everything appeared to be in order. Chick's name was actually entered in the records at Malacanan Palace as consul for Panama, and the officials withdrew, with many bows.

A friendly gardener of Japanese origin struck off a notice to the effect that this was the consulate of Panama. Chick posted this notice on his gate and the Parsons family settled down to a fiction existence, surrounded on all sides by the enemy.

All Manila business houses, as well as prominent residences, were taken over by the invaders and shortly a group of Japanese businessmen offered Chick a job as manager of the manganese and chrome mines of the Islands, some of them his own. They named a big salary, promised him immunity, the use of his motorcar, and freedom to come and go as he pleased. All of which Chick smilingly refused.

"For diplomatic reasons," he explained, "I cannot accept your most generous offer. Besides, I have other things to do."

Just what the nature of these duties might be the Japanese did not inquire, nor did Chick feel it necessary to enlighten them. He had learned, however, that there were unsurrendered soldiers and sailors in the hills of Luzon, still armed with rifles and ammunition; armed, too, with the weapons of the spirit, the spirit of free men.

Very cautiously, working through innocent-appearing peddlers and venders who came to his house. Chick began to inquire into the whereabouts of these men, their numbers, armament, intentions. This slow trickle of information failed to satisfy him. Besides, the placid routine of a diplomat was not to his liking.

"I believe," he confided at last to Katsy, "I'll just slip up there and have a look."

Katsy sighed. "Won't you ever let well enough alone?"

"Probably not." Chick grinned. Chick could, and probably has, gotten away with murder with that grin of his.

Just what he would do with this information, when, as, and if he got it, Chick was not altogether sure. He and Katsy had placed their names on a list of supposed neutrals who wished evacuation to their native shores—and rumor had it that an exchange was in the air. It was possible that he might be able to bring out of the shroud of silence, which now blanketed Manila and Luzon to the world, something of ultimate value.

Presently a barefooted peasant clad in faded garments and a straw hat was on his way to the hills.

In caves and tiny lofty villages at the end of almost inaccessible footpaths Chick Parsons found all kinds of people. Officers whose commands had been annihilated, soldiers who had been cut off from their units in attempting to reach Bataan and Corregidor. Businessmen of Manila who preferred hardship with honor to collaboration without. Farmers and peasants and bandits . . .

There was no unity among these people. No such thing, just then, as an organized resistance or true guerrilla movement. Some were confused and some were dazed, and each man was motivated by a single thought—to protect and maintain himself and his loved ones. The idea of continued resistance had apparently occurred only to a few military men.

All eyes waited upon the sea where President Roosevelt's promised Aid was daily expected.

Chick's secret sallies into the hills were only a germ, the shadow of an idea, and a beginning. These expeditions terminated abruptly on the morning of April 18, 1942, when a Japanese patrol marched into the consulate without knocking or ceremony, arrested Chick, and took him away without explanation.

The Japanese Propaganda radio quickly offered a clue.

Tokyo had been bombed by Doolittle and his B-25s! The unthinkable had happened!

Commentators waxed hysterical, claiming that churches and hospitals had been struck, hundreds of innocent women and children slain. Oriental hatred and fear of the white race flamed quickly to the surface. Every white person appearing on the streets of Manila that day was slapped and kicked by the sentries. Hundreds were arrested by the Kempeitai, or Jap Gestapo. Among them all consular representatives of non-belligerent Caucasian nations.

Katsy and Mrs. Jurika sat at home with the children and waited, as women have waited for their men since time began.

Once before Chick had been arrested and carted off to Santo Tomas to show his papers and explain his business. But this was different. How different Chick will not say, and for two years he did not even tell his wife that he had been in the dungeons of Fort Santiago.

Whatever the Jap inquisitors of Santiago did to this man—and the fingers of his right-hand bear foreshortened nails—it was not enough for their purpose. They could not break his spirit nor secure from him any information of value. In disgust they transferred him to Santo Tomas, the concentration camp, lodging him in barracks still grim with chains and the bloodstains of prisoners who had endeavored to escape and been beaten to death.

From the barracks Chick, through the efforts of a friendly Filipino doctor, was transferred to a hospital in town, where Katsy was able to see him. He was suffering from a mysterious kidney ailment which hinted of the infamous "water cure" of the Japanese, but otherwise he was all of a piece. Presently, through the manipulations of this same physician. Chick was allowed to go home for a week to recuperate.

It was there on the morning of May 29 that he heard of the capitulation of all United States troops in the south and central Philippines and from his own porch helplessly witnessed the humiliation of the heroes of Corregidor.

The lesson, which the curiously warped minds of the invaders expected this dreadful parade through the streets of Manila to teach the people, failed miserably. The people had already witnessed the death march from Bataan in the previous month. While the Filipino soldiers had been carefully spared this brutal treatment and offered amnesty and restoration of full civil rights—providing they would lay down their arms—these Americans, staggering in weakness and delirium through the streets, were friends. Many of them had married into Filipino families, were, in fact, part of the country.

All of them stood for freedom and a democratic way of life which the Filipinos had enjoyed and now so sorely missed.

The Japanese had struck even closer home than this, with the terroristic methods of their secret police, the Kempeitai. Bodies of friends and relatives hung in the squares as reminders that it was necessary to bow three times to each sentry: living Manilans had been chained to pieces of galvanized iron and fried alive in the hot sun.

"What have they done, Mother?" one of the small Parsons boys, coming upon such a scene, asked.

"They struck back at a sentry," Katsy replied.

"Is that bad?"

"Apparently."

"I don't think that's so bad."

"That's because you're not a Jap."

This, then, was the "Orient for the Orientals," was it? This the Co-Prosperity Sphere whose delights the Japanese Propaganda Corps so loudly proclaimed on the air and in the press. This was how it would be?

The soft voices of the people murmured in their blacked-out villages and towns. Now and again one voice, angrier than the rest, was raised—and quickly hushed. General MacArthur had said, "I shall return." There was nothing to do but wait.

"But how long?" the more impatient cried. "When will the Aid come? And is there nothing anyone can do, while waiting?"

"Nothing," replied the elders, who remembered the Spaniards and the suffering, who had learned patience the hard way. The younger ones stirred restively, feeling the yet nameless microbe of resistance moving within them, as it moved within the breasts of the unsurrendered soldiers in the hills. But the time was not yet ripe. The man who would give the first sign that the Aid was on the way, who would produce the leadership and the rifles and the ammunition, was still pacing restlessly up and down behind the barbed wire of Santo Tomas.

Then, without warning, on a night in June Chick Parsons came back from the concentration camp with an armed guard and secret orders. Charles Parsons, consul for Panama, his wife, mother-in-law, and three children, were to prepare at once. They were to pack one trunk, one suitcase. They were to tell no one that they were to be exchanged for Japanese nationals from Latin America.

At the last moment Mrs. Jurika demurred.

"I am not going," she said. "Manila is my home. Besides, my son Tommy has been captured in Cebu."

No argument could sway the older woman. At five-thirty, then, on the morning of June 5, 1942, Chick and Katsy walked out of their home, leaving practically everything they had accumulated over the years. The two older boys were bright-eyed with excitement. It was all a game to them, unpredictable, fascinating. The baby howled for his Chinese amah. The nurse wept and wrung her hands.

Gears clashed, and the truck moved off toward Pier 7.

That afternoon Chick Parsons, his family, and eight other men and women were loaded aboard a hospital ship. No band played them off. Only the screams of desperately wounded Japanese soldiers for whom Manila had no drugs or anesthetics.

Their first destination was Formosa. Beyond that they knew nothing.

In the dark of that first night, as the five of them lay packed in a cabin with blacked-out windows and a guard dozing in the doorway, Katsy whispered a confession that made the sweat spring out on her husband's brow.

During their stay in Manila, for possible future use, the Parsons family had collected various documents. A complete file of the Manila Tribune, Jap-controlled, from the first edition after the fall of the city to the present. Surrender leaflets dropped from the sky into the hills. The names and serial numbers of some three hundred American officers and men imprisoned in camps about Manila.

The latter had been gathered from various sources. A gallant priest, realizing the anxiety of parents and loved ones back in the States whose boys had fallen with Bataan and Corregidor, had brought out a few names from each trip within prison walls. Katsy and Mrs. Jurika had secured others by unobtrusively walking up to Marine and Army prisoners, working on the roads, and asking their names and numbers.

On pain of death, all of the evacuees had been sternly warned by the Japanese not to try to take out of the Islands any material which might be of aid or solace to the enemy. Chick had taken it for granted that Katsy and Mrs. Jurika had destroyed these incriminating documents while he was in the concentration camp.

"It's all here," Katsy now admitted.

"Where?"

"In the little suitcase, under the baby's diapers."

"Dear God," breathed Chick, in anguish and prayer.

From Manila to Takao in Formosa was a five-day sail in the slow hospital ship. An ordeal, instead of the first fine step toward freedom, for Chick and Katsy. Desperately they plotted ways and means of destroying the evidence of these documents, discarded each plan in turn. There wasn't a chance. They were watched day and night. Even their trips to the lavatory were supervised.

"We would gladly have eaten the stuff, sheet by sheet," Chick remarked in retrospect, "but it wasn't possible. We didn't have a single unguarded moment during the entire trip."

Docking at Takao on the west coast of Jap Formosa, the evacuees were herded directly to a great truck, their baggage tossed in after them, the door locked. The truck drove at once to an enclosure, backed up to a large shed. The face of a Japanese customs official—now a member of the local Gestapo—appeared at the opening.

"Inspection," he barked. "Each person stand by own luggage."

Chick sat in the cavern of the truck, staring at the small suitcase. He felt dazed and dismayed. To have brought his family so far and through so much, with freedom just ahead, only to fail at this point, was almost more than he could bear. When the last evacuee had clambered out Chick rose from his seat and gazed hopelessly at the head of the line.

The inspectors were dumping everything in a heap. Their suspicious eyes and nimble fingers were missing nothing.

There was a movement against his leg and, looking down, Chick saw the small face of his four-year-old son Peter gazing up at him. The little fellow seemed to sense that something was wrong, was trying in his childish way to offer help and sympathy.

Chick's eyes jumped from the boy's face to the guilty bag and across the warehouse where a ponderous pillar lent support to the roof. A last desperate chance occurred to him. Not daring to consider how tenuous it might be, Chick knelt by his son.

"You see this bag, Pete?" He tapped the small suitcase. The boy nodded. "I want you to pick it up and very quietly walk over behind that post. Put the bag down, sit on it, and don't move until I tell you."

Peter always did as he was told. Without question he picked up the bag, deposited it in the designated spot, and sat down to await further developments. What these would be Chick had no very definite idea.

Much to his dismay, he now observed two burly Jap sentries approach the boy, squat down, and begin to talk to him in Japanese.

An inquiring glance at Chick, an involuntary nod from his father, and Peter smiled disarmingly at the sentries and replied ... in their own language.

Both the older boys had picked up a bit of Japanese soldier slang in Manila, and Peter promptly began to reveal his talent. This so amazed and delighted the sentries that they reached into their knapsacks and expressed their pleasure by filling the child's hands with candy and fruit.

"Parsons," said a sharp voice behind Chick. "Two-piece luggage. Open trunk first."

Katsy produced the key and watched her careful packing yield to the brutal pawings of the inspectors. Everything was hurled to the dirty floor, then each item returned to the trunk after minute examination. Chick watched the brown fingers turn pockets inside out, run down the seams of dresses. He could feel his wife trembling as she leaned against him, and brushed her arm in reassurance which he did not feel.

"Second piece," barked the chief inspector, slamming the lid on the trunk and chalking it with mystic characters.

"This is it." Chick spoke softly and significantly. As leader of the party he carried a leather portfolio containing the identification papers of the entire group of thirteen. He now thrust this brief case at the official.

The inspector frowned, squinted through thick lenses at the paper in his hand.

"Listing say suitcase," he objected suspiciously.

"Mistake," Chick apologized, bowing. "Small suitcase." He tapped the portfolio. "Brief case."

The inspector hesitated, shrugged his shoulders at the idiosyncrasies of the white race, unzipped the portfolio, and riffled through the papers. Apparently satisfied, he handed the brief case back to its owner.

"Return luggage and persons to truck immediately," he said.

Now came the worst moment of all. It was impossible to leave the uninspected suitcase behind the post. Equally difficult to run it, unobserved, through the gamut of inspectors who lined the avenue of return to the truck. There was only one thing to do.

"Bring the bag, Pete," Chick called. "And come on back to the truck."

The little boy promptly rose to obey. The guards had been very generous with their gifts. Pockets proving inadequate, Pete grappled with his booty and the bag, while grapes ran in all directions and chocolate bars slipped through his fingers to the floor.

The guards let the youngster worry his problem for a moment. Then they swooped down on him, picked up boy, bag and all, in their arms, walked across and deposited the lot in the truck. Just before the door clanged shut one of the sentries patted Peter on the knee and gave him a chattered instruction and final grin.

"What," Chick asked Katsy when he could finally find his voice, "did he tell Pete?"

Katsy was shaking with the hysteria of relief. "He said," she finally managed, "'Next time don't try to carry so much in one trip.'"

Chick wiped his brow.

"Check," he said fervently.

One hundred proof luck, Chick admitted later, was all that saved them in this instance. Once having established itself, their luck held—for their baggage was not again inspected, the Japanese possibly presuming that the only white people on Formosa would not care to go shopping in the middle of a war.

Feeling against all whites was running high on the island at that time. The trip across Formosa from Takao to Taihoku was made in the dead of night, in a private railway car with windows carefully taped. The evacuees were luridly warned as to what might happen to them at the hands of the civilian populace if they made their presence known. They kept well out of sight, especially when quartered in a hotel near the railway station at Taihoku—with the possible exception of young Mike Parsons.

Having inherited the adventuresome spirit of his father, and irked at confinement, Mike escaped under pretense of attending to nature and wandered over to a nearby ballgame—whence he was recovered by a terrified guard and restored to the bosom of his shaken family.

That afternoon the evacuees were loaded into a sealed truck and started on their way again. When released from their temporary prison, they found themselves at an airport—and in a different atmosphere.

The sullen, suspicious attitude of their guards relaxed with the removal of the threat of civilian intervention. The commandant of the Air Force welcomed them into his inner office, produced candy for the children and a couch for baby Patrick's nap. In due time the hum of motors warming up was heard and the evacuees were led out onto the airstrip where a familiar-looking plane awaited.

"Why, it's a Douglas Airliner," Chick remarked involuntarily.

The commandant's smile began to fade.

"The consul from Panama has ridden in the American planes?" he inquired softly.

"Now and then," Chick confessed. "Of course."

"And under what circumstances," said the commandant, his eyes glinting, "from where to where?"

"Manila to the summer capital at Baguio," said Chick calmly. "To escape the heat."

"Ah yes." The commandant seemed relieved. "Then the honorable consul and his family will probably not object riding to Shanghai in this inferior machine which the cowardly Americans abandoned in their headlong flight before our forces?"

"It will be a pleasure." The officer bowed. "Please to remember," he said in conclusion, "to tell the President and people of your honored country the truth about Japanese hospitality."

"I'll do that, amigo," said Chick, grinning.

The commandant shook the hand of the man who was to become Public Enemy Number One to the Jap forces in the Philippines, bowed three times, and shut the door. . .

"This time," said Lieutenant Commander Parsons, USNR, as he buckled the strap about him as instructed by the Japanese flight attendant, "I think the Parsons family is really on its way."

To Chick and Katsy, Shanghai was a lovely derby; the good food, hot baths, and complete release from anxiety. After a couple of weeks of relative bliss they embarked on the Conte Verde for Singapore and then to Lourengo Marquesin Portuguese East Africa. Here they were exchanged for Japanese nationals and taken aboard the Gripsholm for New York, via Rio.

Chick found a house for his family in Biltmore, North Carolina, said hello to his mother and father in Tennessee, and hurried to Washington to report. Shortly he found himself in Colonel Evans' office, in Army Intelligence, telling his incredible story—and studying the messages that had come in from the hills of Panay.

"True or false?" he was asked.

Chick confessed he could not be sure. That there were unsurrendered officers and men in the hills of Mindanao, Samar, Panay, Leyte, he had heard. Luzon, he was sure. That the spirit of free men was rising everywhere he was positive. But a true guerrilla movement, and how directed, how armed and how operating, it was impossible to say.

"Unless ..." Chick hesitated.

"Unless what?"

"Unless somebody goes in and finds out. Somebody," he added slowly, aware that he might be giving himself a new assignment, "who speaks the language, knows the country, and looks like a native."

CHAPTER III

IMMEDIATELY THEREAFTER I BEGAN TO WORK OUT A PLAN with the proper department of the Navy for re-entering the Islands in person to accomplish various objectives.

To ascertain the extent of the guerrilla movement in the Philippines—its leadership, armament, and personnel; to introduce into the Islands an Intelligence organization; to set up coast-watcher and radio stations for the purpose of forwarding word of Japanese movements to the proper Task Force commander; to carry supplies to the unsurrendered soldiers and generally to encourage the people of the Philippines in making intelligent and effective resistance to the enemy—these were the many facets of Chick's plan.

Certain officials in Washington shook their heads.

"You're biting off quite a mouthful, Parsons," they reminded him.

Chick smiled. His teeth are strong and his digestion excellent.

This plan was, in general, approved by the Navy. However, inasmuch as the Theater of the Philippines was under the jurisdiction of General Mac Arthur, it could not be handled except through the chief himself. Accordingly the program was forwarded to MacArthur's headquarters in Australia and the services of Commander Parsons offered to head up this or any other project which might be adopted.

Toward the end of 1942 a brief wire was received by the Navy Department.

SEND PARSONS IMMEDIATELY
(Signed) MacArthur

On arriving in Australia, Chick found that increasing numbers of guerrilla messages, directed to General MacArthur, were being received almost daily. All bore similar assurances—that the senders were faithful soldiers of the Philippines, desirous of getting in touch with the commanding general of the Southwest Pacific Theater for the purpose of setting up communications channels.

These messages were answered in plain language. Through a special means of identifying the senders, Chick worked out a secure secret code. Nevertheless there was as yet no general information available as to what was to be found in the Islands, nor to what extent an organized guerrilla movement had been started there.

Despite the fact that he had only just escaped from the Islands, and fully aware of the consequences of capture and recognition by the Japanese, Chick volunteered to go in, contact the guerrillas, and bring out the desired information.

"Do you think you can get away with it?" he was asked.

"I can try."

"Your height and color are about right, but you're pretty husky—for a Filipino."

"I'll pass."

"Suppose you run into the Japs?"

Chick's eyes opened wide. He stated the philosophy to which he was to adhere for the next two years—with varying success.

"I don't intend to run into 'em. I'm not going in as a commando. I'm going in as a spy."

General MacArthur gave his consent. Chick was relieved of all Navy command and told to go ahead. Thus, with an original personnel of one man, was launched Spyron, or Spy Squadron—an organization to which the guerrillas were to owe everything in months to come.

To include the ideas of the Navy with those already worked out by the Army was. Chick found, a relatively simple matter. Operating in complete secrecy, and aided by the highest priorities, he began to gather supplies for his trip—a trip which he had decided should be made by submarine as a plane was too vulnerable and would attract too much attention.

The ordinary submarine carries its crew, torpedoes, ammunition for the deck guns, and nothing much else—except food. The amount of supplies which could be transported by such a unit was, of course, extremely limited. No bride ever planned her honeymoon packing with greater care than Chick did the space allotted him aboard an operational sub, which would deviate from ordinary war patrol only long enough to land him and his equipment.

Number One Priority Chick gave to signal equipment, consisting of several radio stations of sufficient power to reach Australia, and a number of smaller sets for work within a limited territory. Plus batteries, generators, and spare parts.

It was felt certain that the people would lack medical supplies, and as much atabrine, quinine, and other medicines as possible were loaded on Number Two Priority. In this category also fell arms and ammunition, an assortment of Quartermaster supplies of food and clothing, and limited quantities of "morale builders"—American cigarettes, gum, chocolate bars, and magazines.

At the end of the list Chick placed a fifty-pound can of wheat flour.

"For Communion wafers," he said. The Filipinos are ninety-five per cent Catholic.

While the actual destination was being debated the Australian coast patrol picked up a small open sailboat in which an unsmiling young American officer and two companions had fought their way from Mindanao.

This was Captain Charles Smith, now lieutenant colonel in charge of the Military District of Samar, and a man destined to play an important role in the guerrilla movement of the Philippines. Smith had made this perilous voyage to acquaint General MacArthur with the free movement now being organized in southern Mindanao by Wendell W. Fertig, fugitive from Bataan, and to request radio equipment and supplies to further this movement.

"Mindanao it will be," Chick decided. He had already looked with favor upon this island as his destination, not only because of its size and relative importance in the group but because the coastline was indelibly etched on his brain, due to his former business activities there. Captain Smith was invited by Chick to join the party. Two Moros were taken along because of their knowledge of terrain and dialect.

Late in February 1943, with his supplies stacked snugly in the forward and after torpedo rooms, Chick Parsons came aboard and saluted the bridge of the submarine. The crew cast off, the Diesel-turned screws spurned the safe waters of the harbor. Anti-submarine nets parted and closed over the wake.

The Aid for which the Filipino people had so long prayed was on its way.

The trip, according to Chick's mental log, was fairly uneventful. A few torpedoes loosed against careless Japanese shipping. A few depth charges received in return. All very routine.

Arriving at destination in the manner previously described, Chick decided to go ashore under cover of darkness and contact the local forces. If these were found to be loyal, small fishing boats known as vintas and flying previously agreed-upon signals would be sent out the following afternoon to take delivery of the supplies. If anything happened to Commander Parsons, Captain Smith would continue the mission in the sub and make a landing at another site.

Fortunately this was not necessary as everything went along according to Hoyle. The local forces were found to be members of one of Fertig's outposts. After due apologies for the jitteriness of some of the soldiers which had resulted in our preliminary shower of bullets and the assurance of the commanding officer that it had been done without his orders, we were given the grandest reception it is possible to imagine.

Headquarters in Australia had argued long and persuasively that Chick, in traditional spy fashion, should adopt some disguise. It was pointed out that, should he fall into the hands of the enemy and be identified, not only as a United States naval officer but as the "ex-consul for Panama," he could expect little or no personal consideration.

It was not Chick's intention to encounter the Japanese if he could help it. Besides, instinct and knowledge of the Filipinos caused him to refuse any visual change of character, and an event immediately proved that his reasoning was sound.

The landing spot was purposely chosen for its wild and remote nature. Yet one of the first persons to come down and meet him on the beach was an old lavandera, or washerwoman, who had formerly worked for Commander and Mrs. Parsons in Zamboanga.

"Por Dios, el Chico," the old lady screamed, and fell upon him, broadcasting his identity to the world at large.

No disguise, Chick now realized, could have concealed him from the sharp eyes of this old friend and servant. She would have known him anyway—in which case the attempted ruse would only have confused the local guerrillas and perhaps aroused their suspicions as to the true purpose of his mission.

This fact Chick now tabbed and tucked away in the only notebook he ever carried, the back of his mind. At no time thereafter did he ever adopt a disguise, preferring to have the people recognize him for what he was—an American officer and messenger from MacArthur—and counting on his ability to "blend in" with the country to escape notice of the Japanese.

The reception over—and it was difficult to prevent the ecstatic people from holding an enormous fiesta in his honor, despite the proximity of Jap garrisons only a few miles away and the imminence of wandering patrols—Chick turned tithe matter of securing vessels for the transfer of his supplies.

Learning of his desire, the local guerrilla leader beckoned him to follow and set off toward a nearby stream. Here, presently, Chick found himself gazing at a veritable fleet, hidden away by palm branches in the deep river. A sixty-foot launch powered by Diesels, two or three gas launches, a small lighter, and various other surface craft rode at anchor.

"Where in the world did you get all these boats?" Chick inquired.

"Gift from the Japanese," the guerrilla laughed, drawing significant hand across his throat.

This flotilla, flying the proper security signals, the following afternoon shoved boldly out toward the rendezvous point. At the hour agreed upon the submarine walloped up out of its lair, and both crews stared at each other in mutual admiration and wonder.

"If this is a sample of the guerrilla Navy, I guess you've got something, Chick," said the sub captain, adding to his men: "Okay, boys, heave the stuff up on deck. Commander Parsons wants to get his business started and it looks as though he's going to have plenty of customers."

The supplies were quickly transferred from sub to launch. Captain Smith went ashore with the load. Chick thanked his erstwhile host for a pleasant voyage.

"When shall we two meet again?" inquired the captain.

"Few weeks," said Chick.

"Optimist," smiled the captain, giving the signal to get under way. "You've got a big island and a big job, Chico."

He was right, on all counts. Not for six months was Chick Parsons to see that or any other United States submarine again.

Chick's original landing was accomplished without enemy interference—but not without enemy notice. Even as the submarine disappeared into the protection of the deep, agents from the village were speeding toward Cagayan, nearly one hundred miles away. Within twenty-four hours. Chick later learned, information reached the enemy to the effect that not one, but six large cargo-carrying submarines had dumped thousands of tons of supplies and hundreds of personnel on the beach.

This exaggeration was due, of course, to the desire of the agents to make their mission and information sound more impressive, and caused considerable stir in the Japanese garrison. By the time a punitive force reached the landing spot there was nothing to be seen but a few charred embers of fires and a litter of American cigarette butts, smoked down to infinitesimal proportions.

Guerrillas, villagers, the two American officers, and the supplies had melted away into the hills above Oroquieta, where Lieutenant Colonel Fertig had his headquarters.

Wendell Fertig, West Virginian born, was a mining engineer. Like so many peacetime American residents of the Islands, he held a reserve commission. With the attack on Pearl Harbor he was ordered to Bataan, where he served until the fall of the peninsula to the Japanese. Making his escape by plane to Mindanao, he offered his services to Major General Sharp—who promptly put him to work training young Filipino recruits. At the surrender of Sharp and the USAFFE forces of the south, Fertig took to the hills. A number of officers and men went with him to form the nucleus of what was. Chick now found, a rather impressive guerrilla organization.

"How many rifles can you claim?" Chick inquired. "Five hundred?"

"Five thousand," Fertig corrected him.

"H'm." Chick nodded in approval. "What proportion, rifles to men?"

"One to three."

In the Army the man and his rifle are counted as one unit. In guerrilla warfare the rifle, which can be used constantly, twenty-four hours a day, is the important factor. Men must rest. The rifle never sleeps.

"How are you organized?"

"Roughly, into districts throughout the island. My staff men are in the field."

"That's where they ought to be. Who have you got?"

Fertig named them. Bowler, Wilson, Hedges, MacLish—former Manila businessmen and reserve officers, many of whom Chick knew personally. Morgan . . .

Fertig frowned.

"Who's Morgan?" Chick wanted to know.

"Morgan, a white mestizo, and Tate, a Negro mestizo, started the movement on Mindanao," Fertig said. "Neither of them seems to know what it's all about and they're always fighting. Tate's practically dropped out of the picture. I thought I could handle Morgan better if I gave him a place on my staff, but he won't take orders, claims he's of equal rank—it's 'Colonel Morgan,' by the way, if you ask him—and raises hell with the Moros."

Chick made a mental note to take care of "Colonel Morgan" when the time came and continued to gather from Fertig a picture of the situation in other parts of Mindanao. To the south, in the Lanao region, he was told, Hedges was doing a fine job with the difficult and fiery Moros up around Mindanao.

To a man named Pendatun had a potentially powerful group of unsurrendered soldiers, young recruits, and Moros, but so far had proved uncooperative with Fertig, since he had assumed the rank of brigadier general and claimed he was of equal rank. Farther up the coast MacLish of Fertig's staff had a seasoned group of guerrilla officers and men. To the east under Major Robert Bowler were guerrilla forces of which Fertig knew little, since communication by letter and runner involved weeks.

Mindanao, second largest island in the Philippines group, is divided into Oriental Misamis and Occidental Misamis. Roads are few, much of the terrain is mountainous, and distances are great. The time required to go overland from eastern to western Mindanao takes, roughly, three weeks. Despite this the movement in Mindanao had apparently gained more ground than anyone in General MacArthur's headquarters believed possible.

Chick saw immediately what needed to be done. When Fertig had completed his picture he summed it up: "In other words, these men need arms and ammunition. They need to be brought under one roof and connected by communication with each other and with GHQ in Australia. They especially need to recognize one leader who will take his orders by communication from General MacArthur."

Fertig nodded.

"Okay," said Chick. "I'll get the supplies in to you as fast as I can, starting as soon as I get an over-all picture of Mindanao and the nearby islands. You can set up two of these radio stations we brought in, right away. I'll help all I can, by personal contact, to bring the more powerful independent groups into line. The little bands may be expected to join in automatically, after your command is recognized."

"My command?" Fertig raised his eyebrows.

"Why, sure." Chick smiled. "From what Captain Smith told General MacArthur and me of you and your activities, we had a hunch that you were the right man for the job. From what I've seen and what you've told me in the past few days, I'm convinced. Your appointment as leader of the Tenth Military District of Mindanao will be confirmed immediately by radio with GHQ.

You can spread the word by radio and runner to the other groups that as soon as they recognize your authority their forces will become a party of the United States Army in the Philippine Islands." Chick brought a set of silver eagles from his pocket. "Colonel Fertig, you're in the Army again. Or should I say—still?"

Visibly moved, the colonel pinned on the insignia.

"I'll do my best," he said simply.

"I know you will," said Chick.

Confirmation of the appointment was merely routine, for MacArthur had given Commander Parsons full authority to recognize the leader of a movement on any of the Islands, as soon as he could produce proof that he was capable, sincere, loyal, willing to take orders, and supported by a sufficient group of men sworn to submit to his direction and discipline.

"I'll now give you your first order from General MacArthur," Chick continued. "Under no circumstances are your men to go out in open warfare against the Japanese. Harass the enemy, ambush his patrols, watch his every move on land and sea—but don't engage him in battle or go against his garrisons. You can't hope to win with your present armament of old Enfields and Springfields. You'll only bring reprisals and suffering to the people.

"The time will come," Parsons added prophetically, "when your boys can shoot all the Japs their hearts desire. That time—and it may not be as far off as you think—is when the invasion forces hit the beach."

CHAPTER IV

I HAVE MANY MORE TIMES BEEN FIRED UPON BY friends than by the enemy.

The northernmost point of the island of Mindanao is Surigao. Across a narrow passage of blue water and just to starboard lies the little island of Dinagat. To port is even smaller Panaon and above it Leyte. Between these islands runs the most vital sea lane in all the south and central Philippines—Surigao Strait.

No Japanese ship could move through this strait without observance from the headlands of either Surigao, Dinagat, or Panaon. One of these locations, Chick decided, was a natural for a coast-watcher radio station. So when he had completed his original interview with Colonel Fertig and inspection of his setup, Chick turned to this next project.

At his disposition Colonel Fertig placed one of his most prized possessions, the Nara Maru, a sixty-foot Diesel-Mitsui launch which the guerrillas had wrested from the enemy. Days of weary plodding through jungle and over mountain trails thus avoided, Chick was in a happy frame of mind as he started forth to set up a radio station on Surigao, if possible, and to case the adjacent islands.

Hugging the shore of Mindanao and cruising almost entirely at night to avoid enemy patrol launches, the launch at length put in to Medina on the north coast to refuel and pick up personnel to man the proposed station. This was the headquarters of Ernest MacLish, one of Fertig's district commanders and, with the recognition of the guerrilla movement in Mindanao, newly commissioned lieutenant colonel.

Lieutenant Colonel MacLish, Chick discovered, had a smart organization of young Americans and Filipinos who, before receiving contrary orders from Colonel Fertig, had moved against the Japanese garrison at nearby Butuan—with considerable initial success. The enemy had been driven out and a number of soldiers freed from the Butuan prison camp.

"However," MacLish now confessed ruefully, "the Nip came back in such force that we had to retire."

"Your boys have had their baptism of fire, anyway," Chick observed. "They'll know what to do when the proper time comes."

With the obvious shortage of Diesel fuel, Commander Parsons had wondered how the guerrillas could hope to continue operation of such a launch as the Nara Maru—and here at Medina he made the first of many subsequent observations of guerrilla initiative in full play. For the personnel of MacLish's "service company" were hard at work distilling coconut oil, which, while it does not give the number of B.T.U.s of ordinary fuel, was found to be a worthy substitute—clean-starting, even cleaner burning, and completely satis-factory to drive Diesel launches.

"I never thought the coconut would go to war," Chick laughed.

"It's all things to all men down here," MacLish told him. "Clothing, food, and drink for man or motor. We even drive our trucks and the motors for our battery generators with an alcoholic distillation of the palm flower called tuba." And he showed Chick how the guerrillas nip off the bud at the top of a palm, collect about a quart of yeasty sapper day, and ferment it: then extract the alcohol by using Socony can stills with bamboo tubes running beneath a stream for condensation. "It's not high-test and it's not Old Grandad but it'll get you there, or get you drunk."

"No ration card needed, either." Chick smiled, making mental note to in-clude in his next shipment of supplies a small copper still whose possibilities he had already investigated in Australia.

Most gratefully MacLish received the supplies which Chick now portioned out to him. Further to show his appreciation, he turned over to Commander Parsons not only the personnel he desired to man the coast-watcher station but also the only .50-caliber machine gun in the area.

"It has no recoil spring," MacLish apologized, "and is capable of single shot only. But the boys think they can fix that."

Returning presently to the Nara Maru, Chick discovered the machine gun proudly mounted on the cabin roof with a quite adequate recoil spring installed, consisting of a piece of inner tubing.

"That's fine, Colonel," he thanked MacLish. "But I'm not looking for trou-ble."

"You'll probably find it," said MacLish—and he was right.

Putting ashore well below the town of Surigao, Chick was informed by friendly natives that the Japanese not only held the region completely but had installed their own observation post overlooking the strait. They were also using Surigao as a base for the operation of patrol launches which were even now looking for him, having been informed of his intentions by their efficient espionage system.

Chick was now faced with the alternative of going across to Panaon or, if of his were similarly occupied, up to Leyte—neither of which choices struck him as eminently satisfactory. He wished to place the station on Mindanao, where it would be controlled, administered, and disciplined by Colonel Fertig—thus keeping together the entire Mindanao guerrilla group.

No other course being open. Chick set sail for Panaon. By hiding the launch in the mouth of a stream by day and watching their chances, the party was able to creep across the narrow strait, under the very eyes of the patrols, and make a landing—the first of a friendly nature since the surrender.

Here Chick was greeted by a force of guerrillas who, as the launch sailed in in the dawn, appeared to be smeared with a curious yellow war paint. On closer inquiry. Chick learned that most of the guerrillas in the area were suffering from tropical ulcers. A large enemy mine had floated ashore in the vicinity and, casting about for ways and means of arresting their sores, they had decided to see if the mine might not contain something of benefit.

Calmly taking out the detonators—a process which Chick for all his experience confessed he would not have attempted—they removed the explosive. This powder was found to be high in picric acid and a very fair panacea for the treatment of this type of ulcer.

These mottled guerrillas now swarmed aboard the launch, having been informed of its approach and offering no opposition, and eagerly fell upon the tangible manifestations of American friendship which Commander Parsons produced. Good-naturedly submitting to a reception of the size and enthusiasm which had been accorded him a few days before on Mindanao, Chick finally managed to tear himself away and devote his attention to the more serious business at hand.

Panaon is extremely small, its people almost completely agricultural. The Japanese, beyond a small garrison at Pintuyan, had not bothered to fortify it at this time. On the east coast of this tiny island Chick finally found an ideal site, giving a broad panorama of the strait.

"This is it," said Chick, gazing out at what he would have no way of knowing was to be the scene of the terrific sea battle of October 25, 1944. He sized up the young officer, Truman Hemingway, whom he had brought along to put in charge. "You realize what you'll be up against here, Hemingway? This is one of the hottest spots in the Islands."

The boy nodded.

"The Japs are right across this mountain, in Pintuyan. There's hardly any place to hide around here. And while I'm going over to Leyte to try and arrange to have you supplied with food, you and your boys will have to operate on your own, without adequate guerrilla protection."

"I'll carry on," said Hemingway, "as long as I can."

Neither of them realized at the time just how long Hemingway would carry on without relief, sending out regular word of sea traffic in the strait even while Leyte and Panaon itself were overrun with the enemy. Chick picked his men carefully for this extremely hazardous and vital duty. Some of them were to blow their tops and some to lose their lives, but few would let him down. Hemingway was of the best.

"Good boy," said Chick, and turned toward Leyte.

Here we made, through misunderstanding, an error which might have proved costly.

The Nara Maru was still, to all intents and purposes, a Japanese launch. The Rising Sun flew at the masthead, was painted on deck and reproduced on boards hung over the side. Chick and his party had ridden at sea in this manner to fool any passing patrol plane. Approaching friendly territory, such as Panaon was presumed to be—and Chick always presumed he would meet friends until indications proved otherwise—the Stars and Stripes were run up in place of the Rising Sun, the outboards removed, and a coil of rope placed over the deck flag.

The course now lay around Leyte and through Panaon Straits, a body of water not over a hundred feet across, running between the two islands. Chick had no idea what he would find in Leyte. Aware that it was virgin territory so far as a friendly launch was concerned and that any launch regardless of markings would be viewed with suspicion, the commander put in to a spot below a town on the southern end of the island and cautiously reconnoitered.

He found that guerrillas were on hand and the local officer offered to send runners to the northern end of the island to the garrison commander there, to insure safe passage of Chick's party through the strait.

"Just last week," the leader recalled, "our men caught a Jap in the passage, sank the launch, and killed everyone aboard."

"It's a good thing we landed here, then," said Chick.

Feeling quite safe, Commander Parsons pushed on up the coast to the mouth of the strait.

"Shall we go right on through. Commander?" the helmsman asked.

Chick glanced at his watch. There was plenty of time. Why not say hello to the garrison commander?

"Head for the town dock," he therefore ordered.

The Nara Maru proceeded to sail on in ... to a heavy volley of rifle fire, from troops apparently deployed on the beach. The launch was struck in several places, fuel bubbled to the deck from drums perforated by the bullets, but miraculously nobody aboard was hit.

This was disconcerting to say the least, but Commander Parsons realized there was only one thing to do—keep the launch on its course. If they turned and made a run for it, it would only indicate to the guerrillas that the vessel was what they suspected it to be in the first place—an enemy. Continued fire and of a more accurate nature would be the result.

The unswerving course of the launch appeared to bring pause to some of the men on shore, as did the fact that the American flag flew overhead. The second round came from a rather limited number of guerrillas and the third was only a scattered shot or two.

At this point two of the braver—or more foolhardy-members of the crew ran to the bow of the boat and shouted:

"Stop! We are friends!"

The Nara Mam then proceeded into the pier and was met by a very apologetic young lieutenant who begged forgiveness for firing on friendly forces, the first as a matter of fact to land on Leyte since the surrender.

"Didn't you get word of our approach from the commanding officer of the southern end?" inquired Chick, who was not yet so accustomed to being fired upon by nervous guerrillas as he later became.

"Yes, Commander," said the lieutenant. "We received a message." He held out a guerrilla communiqué. Chick read:

Look out for a launch arriving this afternoon.

"The only launches we are familiar with in these waters are Japanese," the officer explained.

In passing from one pony-express runner to another, customarily stationed two miles apart, Chick deduced, the message had lost some of its original intent. By the time the officer in command of the forces overlooking the strait had received and scribbled it down, only the bare fact of an approaching launch remained.

"What caused you to decide to come in here before proceeding through the strait?" the lieutenant now inquired.

"We were ahead of schedule and thought we'd like to have a look at your setup. Why?"

"Because," said the officer, perspiring visibly, "I have only one fourth of my men in town. The rest are posted there." He motioned toward the heights frowning down upon the narrow strait. "Had you tried to go through without first contacting us . . ."

It was Chick's turn to mop his brow. The Nara Maru would undoubtedly have been sunk and everybody aboard killed, if they had tried to run the strait without stopping.

Luzon, Cebu, Mindanao, Samar, Negros, Palawan, Panay, Mindoro, Leyte . . .

Thus the largest of the 7,000-odd Philippine Islands. Leyte's size is far from commensurate with its importance in the guerrilla movement, and completely dwarfed by its place in the history of American fortunes of war.

Chick Parsons could not know this, however, when he landed in the town of Maasin in southern Leyte in March 1943. Like everyone else, Jap and Filipino included, he presumed that when the landing of American forces was made it would be in Mindanao. Chick only knew that it was up to him to organize and equip the guerrillas on every island to the highest possible degree prior to invasion—and on Leyte he now ran into his first serious problem.

He immediately found that there were a number of guerrilla outfits on the island, both good and bad. Some of these were led by keen, hard-fighting, aggressive young Filipino officers. Others were headed by swashbuckling opportunists whose sights were raised no higher than the objective of eliminating the nearest rival. All of them needed to be brought under one strong, recognized leader.

The Japanese, Chick immediately determined, had practically no forces on Leyte at that time, probably not over three hundred in all. These soldiers were grouped in two garrisons, one at Ormoc on the west coast, the other at Tacloban on the east. Lack of competition, Chick guessed, as much as personal jealousy doubtless caused the rivalry between the two most prominent warring groups in the south. One was led by a yeoman who had been attached to the Sixteenth Naval District at Cavite before the war; the other by a mining engineer who had lost one job after another in the Philippines. Both these men were, in Parsons' opinion, the type to take advantage of a situation, gather together a few rifles, and give their supporters poor leadership.

Almost daily pitched battles occurred between the forces of "Captain" Gordon Lang and "Major X," as Chester Peters, the other leader, called himself. The day before Chick arrived a senseless encounter between the two rivals had resulted in the death of forty-five fine young guerrilla soldiers and the wounding of Peters. Something, Chick saw at once, must be done to avoid further loss of valuable manpower.

Visiting "Major X" first of all. Chick found him to be a boastful swashbuckler, with a mestiza wife who called herself "Joanne of Arc," completely intent on his sole purpose of eliminating the immediate opposition of Lang.

"I'm going to get that guy if it's the last thing I do," he said—and would listen to no suggestions of an armistice in the higher interests of the guerrilla movement, except to add: "If you can get Lang to give up and take orders from me I'll head your movement. I'm the better man anyhow."

Lang seemed to be slightly more amenable to reason, but told Chick: "I've just got to get Peters before he gets me. That's all."

Sensing that neither of the personalities involved in this feud was of sufficient character to head up the guerrilla movement on Leyte, and with the realization that there was no place for personal animosities in such a broad-reaching and potentially powerful program as was planned for the guerrillas, Chick left the young hotheads to their grievances and turned his eyes elsewhere.

They fell, at length, upon one of the highest-ranking officers of the Philippine Army, former district commander for the Army at Samar and Leyte— Colonel Ruperto K. Kangleon.

In his business dealings with all kinds of people in the Philippine Islands Chick had made a host of friends and acquaintances. Here on Leyte he encountered two of these, men of national prominence, the Cuenco brothers. One was a former representative, the other an ex-cabinet secretary. In their eyes there was only one logical person to head the guerrilla movement on Leyte—and accordingly Chick made his way to the farm of Colonel Kangleon at San Roque, on the southern tip of the island.

Here he found the colonel, surrounded by his family, resting from the ordeal of imprisonment at the Butuan camp on Mindanao, from which MacLish's men had released him. Colonel Kangleon received Commander Parsons with customary Filipino hospitality and grace. He listened with the greatest of interest and attention to Chick's plan for the guerrilla movement in the south and central Philippines. But when Chick asked him to take over the fortunes of Leyte the colonel shook his head.

"I am very tired, Commander," he stated. "My health is not of the best. I wish only to rest here with my wife and children."

"No one else knows the country as you do," Chick pointed out. "The soldiers hold you in the highest respect."

"Thank you, Commander, for those gracious sentiments," said the colonel. "But I am weary of war. I am also disgusted with the actions of some of my countrymen on Leyte—and of yours."

"You have heard about Lang and Peters, then?"

"Who has not? I see no sense in guerrilla fighting guerrilla when the real enemy is the Japanese."

"Exactly," Chick agreed. "Someone must put an end to this idiotic striving of little group against little group for the leadership of perhaps two hundred rifles. There is only one man in Leyte today who can do that—and the Cuenco brothers share my opinion."

"Ah?" The colonel raised his eyebrows. "You have talked with los Cuenco?"

"I have. In fact I have come directly from them to you."

The colonel frowned.

"I am not young, Commander Parsons. I think this is a job for a young man."

"On the contrary, it is a job for a man who has the full support not only of the soldiers but of the civilians. Without the latter no guerrilla movement can operate successfully. Once a leader gets on the outs with the civil populace a Japanese patrol has a way of mysteriously learning of his whereabouts, and his days are numbered."

"True."

"When I return I hope to start a stream of rifles flowing in to the Islands without letup until each guerrilla—not just one in three—has his own carbine or tommy gun."

"Many of the men are using old Enfields, Springfields, captured Jap rifles, homemade shotguns," the colonel reminded him.

"Ammunition of every kind will be brought in."

"The guerrillas are refilling shells with the powder from duds mixed with Chinese firecracker powder; they are using tinfoil, potash permanganate, and matchbox scrapings for fuses. . . ."

"Powder, caps, fuses are on the list. Radio stations, generators, motors, medicines. . . ."

The colonel stared at Chick's earnest face in wonder.

"You believe you can bring in all these things, by underwater craft, in amounts sufficient to be worthwhile?"

"I do," said Chick quietly. "General MacArthur and Vice-Admiral Kinkaid are squarely behind me and the organization I am about to set up. The Army will secure, under highest priorities, the specialized equipment the guerrillas need. The Navy will transport this materiel, and not just in occasional operational submarines diverted temporarily from patrol. It is my hope in time to have a fleet of cargo-carrying submarines assigned wholly for this purpose."

The colonel's eyes began to flash.

"These supplies will not be given to wildcat guerrilla bands to enable them to knock each other off more effectively. They will only be sent in to areas where a good and true guerrilla movement is under way."

"And how do you determine the quality of such a movement?"

Chick played his ace.

"A guerrilla movement is just as good as its leader," he said.

Colonel Kangleon looked out over the land he loved so well, which he had served so long and faithfully, calling to him now through the persuasive voice of this true friend of the Filipino people. Slowly he rose.

"Apparently it is not the time for a soldier to rest," he said slowly. "You have made my duty clear, Commander Parsons. I have no choice. You may tell General MacArthur that I am at his disposition."

Satisfied that the destiny of the guerrilla movement in Leyte was in the right hands, Chick now turned back toward Mindanao. On the way he decided to drop in on the town of Malitbog, on Leyte's south coast, to see what the situation might be in that region and also to spread word that the Aid was coming.

While yet a long way off, he could see the people making for the mountains as was customary whenever a strange launch appeared. By the time the vessel got within hailing distance of the pier the town of fifty thousand was completely empty—except for a few troops of guerrillas deployed about the beach.

These guerrillas, Chick found, while extremely nervous and completely ready to engage whatever force might come off the launch, withheld their fire. This, he learned, was the new technique, precluding the possibility of the launch turning away at the first far-range volley. The fact that Chick's party was largely white was also a factor which caused the guerrillas to cogitate and hold fire.

Rapidly learning the hard way, Chick did not make the mistake of walking toward the guerrillas when the launch docked, but waited until the bolder ones came to him. When it was found that the party was friendly there was great rejoicing. Runners immediately went to the hills to indicate that an American representative had come to the Islands and to this town for the first time.

Due to the frequent forays of the Japanese, the people of the lower Philippine Islands have added, with grim humor, an American word to their vocabularies. This is the word "evacuate." Chick's young American guerrillas did not take long to note the similarity between the Filipino pronunciation of this word—which they called "e-bac-whit"—and that of "buckwheat." The return is called balikuate, a Visayan word. The Visayan language is spoken in central and southern regions.

"Buckwheat" and "balikuate" thus have become standard expressions for an activity which is almost as common to the Filipino people as our washing the hands. A daily, and sometimes oft daily, occurrence.

When the good news reached the hills the people began to balikuate with far more celerity than they had "buck-wheated." Their natural curiosity was whetted by the visible evidence that Chick's party had come from outside and from friendly sources. This evidence, in the form of cigarettes, chocolate bars, and medicine, Commander Parsons now began to unload and distribute.

The joy of the people was tremendous. Some laughed, some danced, others cried. Many of the women threw their arms about Chick's young officers and kissed them ecstatically—for this was the first manifestation most of them had had that the Yanks really were coming.

As usual the town wanted to hold a fiesta in honor of the great occasion. However, Chick knew that the success of this, as of his other missions, depended on mobility. There was no telling when the Japs might appear or from what direction, and the sixty-foot launch tied up at the pier was a sitting duck.

Chick spent only an hour or so in the town, securing the information he desired, and returned to the dock, where he was tended a reception which would have been ludicrous if it had not been so pitiful and sincere.

Waiting on the end of the pier stood the mayor and his entire staff, clad in prewar finery. Some of these costumes had obviously come from the bottom of trunks, and some had even been dug up out of the ground. Creases ran every which way and a hasty brushing had not sufficed to compensate for long disuse.

With the entire populace lined up on shore, the mayor stepped forward.

"Commander," he said, hand outstretched, "welcome to Malitbog and to a very grateful people."

With that, the mayor completely disappeared from sight!

The dock was not in the best of repair, and in stepping forward with his eyes on Chick's face. His Honor had not noticed a large hole. He emerged presently from beneath the pier, none the worse for his fall, found the humorous side of the situation, and joined in the general merriment.

Actually this broke the ice and began a friendship which I was to enjoy with this same mayor and in this same town most profitably later on. At the invasion Malitbog and Maasin happened to be the only towns in southern Leyte containing Jap garrisons. The friendship and co-operation of these wonderful people was to aid me immeasurably when I led the guerrilla forces against these garrisons on Dog Day.

When Commander Parsons returned to Leyte with supplies several months later he found that the entire area—barring one small unimportant unit—had come over into Colonel Kangleon's camp. The warring elements had been brought together in harmony, creating a beautiful fighting unit which was well on its way to causing the Japanese worry and casualties, a unit which was readying itself for a major role at invasion time.

Peters and Lang gradually drifted out of the picture. The men they had misdirected quickly yielded to the superior direction and purpose of the colonel and became excellent fighting men.

Chick Parsons has reason, from start to finish, to be proud of his accomplishment on Leyte. A perfect example of the justice of his statement:

"A guerrilla organization is just as good—or bad—as its leader."

CHAPTER V

"IT DID NOT TAKE VERY LONG TO SELL PENDATUN on the idea that I actually did come from the Southwest Pacific headquarters of General MacArthur. A couple of packages of American cigarettes did the trick."

"Brigadier General" Salipada Pendatun, Commander Parsons learned on returning to guerrilla headquarters in Mindanao, did not take kindly to Colonel Fertig's claim that he had been appointed district commander of Mindanao.

It was fairly common for every guerrilla leader, in the early stages of the game, to make claim to be headman of his particular island or district. Furthermore Pendatun's claim was backed up by several thousand-armed men, including many good Moros, whom he had taken up into the rich Del Monte section south of the Cagayan Valley, where he found the economic situation very favorable to the sustenance of his organization.

Somehow someone had to persuade this fiery little chief to come into the fold—and wherever a tough assignment cropped up, Chick Parsons never passed the buck to anyone else.

"I'll see if I can't get that star off his collar," he told the colonel. Colonel Fertig was visibly worried. He had already instructed Lieutenant Colonel Robert Bowler, one of his deputy commanders, to send messages to Pendatun, informing him of the new appointment and asking him to add his groups to those already unified on the island. "It's a dangerous assignment, Chick," said Fertig soberly. "I think I can get through," said Chick.

"I'll radio to have an armed guard waiting for you."

Chick shook his head.

"That would only be asking for trouble. I'll take one guard and go, as usual, unarmed." Wearing his Navy cap and carrying one small knapsack of "morale builders," Chick set out with Bowler and a guide. By observing extreme care and taking a circuitous route of little-used trails, Commander Parsons presently arrived at Pendatun's headquarters without accident.

Rumor had not underestimated the strength of Pendatun's organization. Many of his officers were unsurrendered Americans.

One of them was a retired United States officer, Major Frank Magee, Chief of Staff of Major Edwin Andrews, former chief of Philippine Air Corps. His other staff members, all of whom were grouped about him, were equally impressive: the former governor of Cotabato; one of the head men of the Philippine Air Service; a former senator. In fact Pendatun, a lawyer and member of a provincial board, adviser to the governor, had a better staff than Fertig himself, and he greeted Commander Parsons with no great enthusiasm.

"How do I know you come from General MacArthur?" he inquired haughtily, tapping with his riding crop the cavalry boots he invariably wore.

Chick promptly produced his passport: American cigarettes, a supply of atabrine tablets, some recent issues of Time magazine.

Pendatun opened his eyes.

"This is only a sample," Chick reminded him. "Radio sets, guns, ammunition, and many other supplies will be yours if you will join in with Colonel Fertig."

"And what rank is it proposed that I take?"

"Major."

Pendatun sniffed. "I am a brigadier general," he said loftily. "I have a radio station, a pony express service. I have guns. My men know how to use them, too. Come. I will show you."

It was Pendatun's sworn resolve to engage the Japanese whenever and wherever he found them. He was in the midst of such an endeavor—and to prove to the people of this particular region to which he had just moved that he was a real warrior—when Chick arrived.

It was the custom of the Japanese, in garrisoning certain key towns throughout the south and central Philippines, to pick out the sturdiest building in the area as their fortress. This might be the municipal building—ordinarily of concrete—or the substantially constructed convento of the Jesuit priest. In addition to heavy walls, this building had the added advantage to the Japanese of location in the center of town, surrounded by the entire populace or whatever portion of it had not taken to the hills.

Usually about half the population—civil service employees, tax collectors, post office workers, clerks as well as the older and less adventuresome—remained, carrying on the only jobs they knew.

Such a town was Malaybalay, capital of the province, with a normal peacetime population of ten thousand. To the Japanese garrison, snugly ensconced in the normal school at the upper end of the town, Pendatun now devoted his attention. He refused to listen to Commander Parsons' warning that the knocking out of this particular garrison would only bring reprisals in force.

"My men have already blown up the bridges between this town and the next Jap garrison in Cagayan. When we have eliminated the enemy here we shall proceed against Cagayan. After that, Davao. I intend," he summed up his ambitious plan, "to free the entire area from the Japanese."

Chick decided to hold his tongue. Pendatun deployed his men about the school building and gave the order to fire. Round after round of .30-caliber bullets bounced harmlessly off the concrete. The Japanese shouted derisive taunts and replied with the chatter of machine guns.

Pendatun grew a little red in the face.

"Prepare the bombs and catapults," he shouted.

The guerrillas had constructed catapults from bamboo and inner tubing. Incendiary bombs consisting of beer bottles filled with gasoline, stoppered with a detonator and connected by safety fuse to the outside of the bottle, were lit. The bottles flew through the air and shattered harmlessly against the walls, such of them as reached that far.

"Regular bombs," ordered Pendatun, and Chick was surprised to see the guerrillas dart off into the jungle and return shortly, lugging fifty- and hundred-pound aerial bombs.

"Where in heaven's name did you get those?" he inquired.

"I told you I had everything," Pendatun boasted. "My men found these at the airfield and hid them away at the time of the surrender. A quantity of dynamite detonators were recovered from the gold mines. Now you will see."

The regular detonators of the bombs were removed, the dynamite detonators inserted, and a safety fuse placed in the end of the bomb.

They'll never be able to move those catapults close enough to the building to score a solid hit. Chick thought. The machine-gun fire is too hot.

He was right. The bombs fell short and, while a bit of shrapnel damage was done, the Japs continued to refuse to be dislodged.

Pendatun, old boy. Chick observed to himself, you're on the spot. You've got ten times the men the Japs have but you just can't get at them.

Aloud he said nothing except a gentle:

"A few American mortars, a bazooka or two, perhaps a fieldpiece, General, such as Spyron hopes eventually to get in to the recognized guerrilla leaders . . ." He left the sentence unfinished. Pendatun gave no indication that he had heard, retired into conference with his officers.

"A slight delay, Commander," he apologized. "One of my brilliant young men has had an excellent inspiration. Soon the garrison at Malaybalay will be no more."

Silently, Chick followed the general and his staff to a nearby wallow where a herd of carabao were happily lolling in the mud. The carabao, or water buffalo, is the slow, easygoing work animal of the Philippines, comparable to the American ox.

"We shall strap a hundred-pound bomb on each side of one of these noble beasts," explained Pendatun, "and drive him toward the building with the explosive detonated to coincide with the time of his arrival."

This plan seemed to Chick blithely to ignore several very tangible possibilities—to wit, that the carabao would quite likely stop halfway down the course and peer about for a convenient mud hole or munch a snack of grass.

Retiring behind closed doors, so to speak, the guerrillas thereupon endeavored to cope with these various possibilities. Pacing off a distance commensurate to that from their front lines to the Jap fortress, they timed a few of the more energetic animals over this course. Since no one could actually go along on the test and beat the animal into his top speed, a lope, another stimulating agent had to be found.

When the great moment arrived, and the fastest carabao had been readied with a bomb on each side of his hump, a guerrilla soldier tied a handful of gasoline-soaked rags beneath his tail. The carabao was "aimed." A match was struck.

"Fire," shouted General Pendatun—and the carabao dashed off, bellowing with fright and pain. His pace proved even swifter than anticipated. When the beast was within fifty feet of his objective the bombs exploded—tearing off the front of the building.

The terrified Japanese poured out like ants and made for the hills, where the guerrillas, deployed about all possible retreat routes, were able to eliminate about half of them. The rest escaped to Cagayan.

The reaction of the people of the area, Chick now observed, was extremely favorable. Pendatun became the hero of the hour. He was made, in the Del Monte region, and from that moment received the wholehearted support of the citizenry.

Nevertheless, in further conversations with Commander Parsons the little leader was not quite so boastful, not quite so sure of himself. Chick's words about the benefits of Commander Parsons had apparently struck home. Besides, Chick sensed, it had apparently gone somewhat against the grain of the general to have had his fate balanced precariously on the back of a lowly water buffalo.

Chick pressed this advantage with vigor, indicating all possible benefits inherent in joining forces with Fertig. Finally Parsons' sincerity, plus the magic name of MacArthur and the deep-seated patriotism of this peacetime politician, prevailed over his personal pride and ambition.

Pendatun took off his star, put on the gold oak leaf, and saluted.

In Pendatun and his men Commander Parsons had brought one of the most efficient and versatile of all the guerrilla groups into, the United States Forces in the Philippines. Forthwith he spent several days viewing Pendatun's accomplishments and cleverly mingling praise, which he was able to give quite sincerely, with constructive criticism. Thus he made of the leader both ally and personal friend.

Pendatun's staff had great potential genius. Chick said so, indicating, however, that it was far better for these officers to go into the field and show the men how things should be done than to send critical communiqués from headquarters. This—though Chick wisely refrained from saying so—was Fertig's way, the military method.

Pendatun, a Washingtonian type of official, promised to give it a try.

With verbal satisfaction Commander Parsons reviewed Pendatun's well-drilled cavalry group, his fierce Moro commandos—while pressing home the manner in which General MacArthur wished these guerrillas to harass the enemy rather than make frontal attacks upon him and his strongholds. Secretly Chick sensed that the Japs would return to newly freed Malaybalay and teach Pendatun the lesson he was rather reluctant to learn.

In general it was easy to praise the accomplishments of this energetic little leader, for his men had shown great initiative in meeting their own needs. In relatively secure upland regions they had cultivated farms to produce their own vegetables. They had roving herds of cattle and pigs, flocks of chickens, which were driven along with them—since no guerrilla band of any size could afford long to stay in one place. A portion of the Del Monte pineapple plantation had been salvaged for the immediate use of the guerrillas, as well as for the future. Lacking coconut palms, they had learned to extract alcohol from the mash of the gabi root, or potato.

At the time of the surrender a number of radio operators and engineers had been marooned in the region of the Del Monte airfields. Since Pendatun was the only guerrilla leader in the area at the time, these men had been brought into his forces. They had proceeded to build a powerful radio station, whose electricity they produced in a manner which especially drew the admiration of Chick and appealed to his mechanical bent.

Taking the differential and axles of a truck, they had bolted paddles to the wheel flanges and suspended the device on a platform over a swift mountain stream. Power was transmitted through the differential into the drive shaft, which was hooked up to motor-truck generators to charge batteries to run the radio station and likewise to give electricity and light to the houses and offices of the guerrillas.

When the water was swift an attendant who stayed on duty at all times changed the gear into the proper ratio for the rate of flow of the stream. When low, the gears were correspondingly shifted, maintaining a constant voltage at all times on the light plant and a proper rate of charge for the batteries. Compensation for the different levels of the shaft was made by the universal joint; raising and lowering of the water wheel was accomplished by pulleys suspended from a bamboo tower.

The radio station, thus powered, made it extremely simple to put Pendatun into communication with his superior. Colonel Fertig. It was only necessary to arrange a schedule between the two stations and exchange information as to frequencies—which Chick effected as soon as he had persuaded Pendatun to join up with the district commander.

By the time he was ready to leave Pendatun's area Commander Parsons had advanced his friendship to the stage where it was even possible to josh the dignified little leader and engage in a friendly feud over who was the taller—or shorter—Parsons or Pendatun.

In urging Pendatun not to go out in open warfare against the enemy Commander Parsons was not motivated solely by the wishes of General MacArthur. Better than most he knew the rugged nature of the terrain, the jungle temperament of the average young Filipino fighting man. He had already witnessed at least one example of the helplessness of guerrilla armament against the superiority of Jap arms and on every hand had gathered grim reminders of Jap reprisals against the innocent populace as well as the attacking guerrillas. All this had inclined Chick toward the sniper and ambush type of action as the most effective means of combating the enemy, and each additional day he spent in the Islands made this inclination mount toward conviction.

These sentiments, of course, were not shared by the enemy, who was constantly enraged at having to fight a foe largely invisible, an enemy whose forces were continually whittled down by their inability to cope with a hit-and-run type of warfare so contrary to all their training.

The outraged temper of the Japanese was frequently evidenced by the dumping from the sky upon guerrilla strongholds of leaflets—calling the guerrillas yellow, urging them to come out and fight like men and "like the Japanese soldier, who is not afraid to die for his Emperor."

These leaflets merely furnished the guerrillas, whose sense of humor is very acute, with laughter . . . and toilet paper. In most sections they continued to fight in the only sensible way possible, considering the nature of their country, the superior equipment of their enemy, and the fact that the guerrilla is, after all is said and done, a jungle fighter.

Guerrilla bravery had never been doubted for a moment by Commander Parsons. He was now to witness its displaying the most striking fashion.

In line with his policy of securing as complete a picture of guerrilla activity in a given area as possible. Chick left Pendatun and headed north. Circling Cagayan and the Jap garrison there, he came at length to the camp of one of the most picturesque of the minor guerrilla leaders. Captain Hamid.

Hamid was by birth a Moro and Mohammedan. He wore his hair long and covered with the traditional turban, to which was affixed his insignia of rank. He had been married by a pseudo priest to a Christian girl. Consequently he wore a crucifix. He also commanded a battalion of Christian Filipinos.

Most Filipinos are bamboo artisans and when guerrillas stop even briefly they build small, artistic houses of bamboo thatched with the ever-present nipa palm. Not far from Opol, a town six kilometers west of the enemy stronghold at Cagayan, Captain Hamid had built a beautiful little village of bamboo houses. Rather imposing cottages for the officers and their wives, houses instead of barracks for the men, office buildings and even a chapel completed the picture of comfort and security which now confronted Commander Parsons' eyes.

It was not all peaceful however. Hamid's village was located on a deep mountain stream on one side of the provincial road running from Cagayan to

Davao in the south. American forces, prior to the surrender, had destroyed the bridge and it had not been rebuilt. On the opposite side of the stream the Japanese had dug in similarly but in far less comfort.

Hamid's function of the moment was to prevent the Japanese from coming out of Cagayan into guerilla country.

Occasional rifle fire was exchanged by the two groups, but neither was able to do anything really effective to break the existing state of siege. Ignoring the challenges and insults shouted across the water by the Japanese, this guerrilla chief had settled down to a fairly normal existence—but ready, on the other hand, to resist the enemy and then fade away into the jungles if he should attempt to cross the river in force.

The Moro loves to fight. In the presence of this distinguished representative of a great Navy and a great nation Hamid now proceeded to put on a show—without Commander Parsons' knowledge.

After a bountiful supper, Hamid tightened the sash belt of his whipcord breeches, flicked a few crumbs off his gaudy, wide-sleeved shirt—for he was considerable of a dandy—and inquired softly:

"Will the commandant do me the honor to inspect my front lines?"

It was a beautiful moonlight night. The heavens were thick with stars. The commandant sound save the call of night birds and the murmur of the dark stream. Chick thought a little walk would do him good.

"Lead on," he said.

Like a couple of country gentlemen taking a turn in the garden after dinner, Hamid and Chick proceeded from the village to the river bank, where guerrillas crouched in fox-holes and behind log barricades, watching the opposite shore.

"Just where is the enemy entrenched?" Chick wanted to know, since Hamid was strolling along the bank with all the casualness of a promenader on Broadway.

"Oh, he's over there." Hamid motioned airily across the stream—a matter of a hundred yards. Chick calculated. With considerable relief he followed his host into a curving trench.

"Juan, Pedro, Pepe," Hamid called softly.

Barefooted guerrillas, their eyes gleaming with excitement, came and knelt at attention by their leader's side. Hamid whispered a few instructions, inaudible to Chick, and handed the men something which they quickly stuffed in their shirts. With catlike agility the youngsters climbed over the parapet. The moonlight glinted briefly on their rifle barrels. Then they disappeared from view.

Minutes ticked by while the stream murmured to itself and Chick wondered. Deep in his throat Hamid chuckled.

"You find something of amusement, no?" whispered Chick in Spanish.

"I find something of much amusement," replied Hamid, "but not to el Jap."

As he said this the jungle calm of night on the opposite bank was broken by explosions, as of giant firecrackers. Screams of rage and pain came up from the Jap positions. Machine guns chattered a frantic protest and bullets swam wildly overhead.

Only then did it dawn on Chick that Hamid had ordered number of his men to swim the river, slip up on the Jape placements, and drop hand grenades in the very laps of the Japanese.

"They'll never get away with that," Chick objected hotly. "They can't possibly get back alive."

Hamid yawned. "Patience, Comandante," he said, and added almost immediately, "They are back." He counted the dripping figures who had magically materialized out of the river. "All of them and very much alive."

"Bien hecho," said Hamid to the detail. "Well done. Now resume your posts."

The young guerrillas, looking so childlike with the ragged uniforms clinging to their slight figures, grinned and saluted.

"Gracias, Capitain," they murmured, and Chick could see that they were actually flattered to have been chosen for this dubious mission.

Anyone, Chick decided once and for all time, who thinks the guerrilla soldier is a coward is either a fool—or a Japanese.

The next day he learned that sixteen Japs had been killed by the grenades and a number of others wounded. Only handful, to be sure. Yet all over Mindanao, everywhere throughout the central and south Philippines, the decimating process was going on.

Japanese patrols returning minus a few men . . . Japanese guards picked off emplacements by shadowy snipers. . . Jap trucks ambushed . . .

And this last technique, so dear to the hearts of the guerrillas, so devastating to the methodical Japs, Chick was to observe a few days later on his return to Colonel Fertig's area.

To relieve Jap garrisons and patrols in places available byroad the Japanese employed trucks almost as big as boxcars—customarily used in cane countries like Hawaii and the Philippines, then promptly "disarmed" them by operating on regular and unimaginative schedules in supplying and relieving their personnel.

An important function of guerrilla outposts was to observe the movements of such trucks. Action was withheld, however, until the schedule was familiar—and until the guerrillas were sure a truck would pass a given point at a given time, with a full load of a hundred and fifty soldiers.

The trap was then set.

His arrival at a guerrilla encampment coinciding with the preparation of such an ambush not far away. Commander Parsons went along to witness this phase of guerrilla warfare.

The guerrillas chose a mountainous forest area which would permit them to approach unseen and to retreat with safety if that should become necessary. On one side of the road, behind natural barriers, were placed two or three guerrillas armed with tommy guns and automatic rifles.

"These men," explained the young guerrilla lieutenant, "are to fire into the windshield, tires, and engine, bringing the vehicle to a halt within fifty feet."

"How do you know it will stop within fifty feet?" Chick inquired.

"It always does," was the laconic answer.

Down the road, at this given point, and on the opposite side from the firing squad, the main body of the guerrillas dug a long trench. Covering this with a camouflage of sod and grass, they faded away into the thick jungle underbrush.

There was nothing more to do but wait—for the inevitable.

Chick and the lieutenant retired to a promontory, out of the line of fire but where they were perfectly able to witness proceedings. Objections continued to roll through Parsons' head.

"Why are most of the men hidden on one side of the road only?"

"Because that is the side the Japanese always come out on, the side away from the original volley farther back."

The distant grinding of a large truck echoed through the forest. Chick wasn't yet satisfied however.

"If the truck is armor-plated, why don't the Japs stay inside and fight off the guerrillas?"

"Claustrophobia," said the barefooted lieutenant who had graduated from West Point not so long ago. "Panic strikes the Jap and his only thought is to get out of the truck and behind something immobile where he can return fire. Perhaps you might say he just gets panicky."

"With a short-wave radio," Chick continued with his logic, "I should think the Japs could call for reinforcements and hold off the guerrillas by staying inside until help comes!"

"They could. But they don't. The Japanese are most accommodating. You'll see."

On came the great truck, lumbering and protesting up the grade, plumes of steam spurting from beneath the radiator cap. The three men with "Bars," Browning automatic rifles, on the right-hand side of the road, waited until the peaked caps of the driver and his mechanic were fairly in their sights. Then they let go a burst.

The windshield of the truck cracked and splintered. Tires exploded. The engine gave a death rattle. To a chorus of frightened screams from within the truck staggered drunkenly—came to a halt, exactly where predicted.

Out poured the little men in the green uniforms, to fallen masse into the concealed pit. Other little men clad in any kind of uniform depressed their rifles on the struggling figures below, surged down out of cover with wild yells.

Long bolos gleamed in the sunlight, razor-sharp trench knives rose and fell.

It was all over in a minute. In two minutes not a stitch of clothing or piece of equipment was left on the bodies in the trench and along the road. A few more rifles for the guerrilla arsenal, a few more figures added to the ever-growing total of Jap casualties at the hands of the jungle

Commander Parsons rubbed his eyes in amazement, nodded in approval, and made another mental note.

I am definitely a guerrilla. I see no sense in risking annihilation in open combat when you can fight, kill, run—and, later, fight again.

CHAPTER VI

I LET THE GUERRILLAS DO THE HITTING WHILE I did the running. I became pretty expert at it, though now and again I started a little late. A close call of which I am not at all proud occurred in June 1943, when I was preparing documents for a return to Australia.

Wherever he went in the Philippine Islands, Commander Charles Parsons found the doors of Filipino homes wide-open. Sometimes the home was only a bamboo hut; sometimes it was a mansion of adobe stone. Family circumstances might differ, but the spirit of hospitality and friendship accorded this emissary of freedom was the same throughout.

On the shores of Iligan Bay, which almost succeeds in cutting Mindanao in half, lies the town of Jimenez. Here, in the Spanish casa of the Ozamis family, Chick Parsons basked in the luxury of running water, electric lights, fan, and radio, and briefed his findings.

It was late June, almost four months since he had left Australia, just a year since Chick and his family had been evacuated from Manila. He had covered a lot of territory, in every sense of the phrase.

Much of Mindanao Chick had seen with his own eyes. That the future of the guerrilla movement here would be bright he had no doubt—not only because of the caliber of Fertig, Pendatun, Hedges, and the other leaders, but also because on this vast, almost roadless island the resistance movement had been able to develop with only a minimum of interference from the Japanese, would so continue to grow.

Leyte, with Colonel Kangleon sending almost daily messages of the progress of his command, was another matter for satisfaction—a most pleasing and personal one to Chick Parsons.

Chick had not been able to visit Panay, from whence Macario Peralta had first sent a plea for help groping toward the United States. Nor would he need to later, except to bring in supplies. He had already learned that Peralta had a strong, aggressive force—so distasteful to the Japanese that in May they had invaded Panay in numbers, driven the former attorney to the hills, captured his wife and children.

Peralta's radio was briefly silent. Then it spoke again, indicating to the world that not even the threatened execution of his loved ones could swerve this fiery leader from his resolve; indicating, in other exchanges of messages with Commander Parsons, that Peralta was the unquestioned leader of Panay, that his men were solidly behind him, and that the district might be added to the roster of recognition.

Working at his preliminary report, in a blacked-out room in the second story of the Ozamis house at Jimenez, Chick checked off Panay.

Fertig, Kangleon, Peralta—peacetime leaders who had turned their strength and talents to war—these men guaranteed the future of the guerrilla movement on Mindanao, Leyte, and Panay. In the other important islands of the south and central groups the picture was not so happy as leaders struggled for supremacy.

Bohol, set in the center of Mindanao Sea, Chick had managed to look in upon briefly; too briefly to throw the weight of his authority and persuasion into the contest for authority of the two leaders there, each backed by a considerable number of followers. On Samar and Negros, Commander Parsons had been informed by his agents, a like situation existed. On strategic Cebu the two co-leaders were personally friendly, professionally antagonistic in methods of operation.

"Nevertheless," Chick now recorded, "there are vigorous, potentially able guerrilla groups and leaders in all the important and central islands. The law of survival of the fittest will solve some of these situations. Others I shall endeavor to handle on my next trip. . ."

Chick put down his pen and strolled to the window. Just across the bay, not twenty miles away in the town of Iligan, the Japanese had a patrol launch base. Below the Ozamis house, on the beach, guerrilla guards kept ceaseless vigil, ready at the first sign of approaching danger to sound the alarm.

Commander Parsons went back to his desk.

"Luzon," he wrote, and had just added a question mark when the all too familiar danger signal—the ring of iron on iron—sounded through the town.

The Ozamis family stirred in the house, preparing for the usual evacuation to the hills and safety. The youngest of the pretty daughters of this American-Filipino family tapped at the door.

"Vamos, Chico," she said. "We must leave."

Chick groaned. "Every night we leave for nothing," he objected sleepily. "Those boys down on the beach are too jittery."

"It is better to be jittery than to hang up by your thumbs," the girl reminded him.

Chick looked at his own scarred hands.

"Guess you're right, chica. You go ahead with the folks. I'll catch up with you."

"Okay." She smiled.

Feet padded down the stairs. The door closed. Silence fell on the house of Ozamis and Chick brought his thoughts back to Luzon.

The entire island, outside of Bataan and Corregidor, had fallen very rapidly to the Japanese after Pearl Harbor. Consequently there had been no opportunity in this limited time to recruit, arm, and train a body of men such as was afforded the USAFFE leaders in the south and central sections. Nor were there on Luzon large numbers of unsurrendered soldiers to return home, hide their arms, emerge as vigilantes—and later as true guerrillas.

There were, Chick knew from his own experience, groups of officers and men who had taken to the hills from Bataan, Corregidor, and the Manila region. Just how well organized these groups now were he could not say. The basis for an Intelligence ring, if not for organized resistance, was there, anyhow.

Chick left the enigma of Luzon for the future. Besides, he had learned even more than he had come to find out.

The free movement was not just the faint voice of one unsurrendered officer, sitting up in the hills with a radio station and a few armed henchmen. It was a vibrant, living, growing thing, burningly subscribed to by thousands of young Filipinos and Americans. It had the acknowledgment and support of large segments of the non-belligerent population, lacking only supplies and direction from outside to make it a formidable thorn in the side of the Japanese, a deciding factor in the tide of invasion fortunes.

Everywhere in the Philippine Islands the movement was under way. Now for the Aid—the rifles and ammunition, the radios, the medicines. . . .

Commander Parsons threw down his pen, turned out the shaded lamp by which he had been working, and parted the blackout. All about him the town lay silent, deserted. Little waves greedily licked the shore. There were no signs of the enemy.

The bed in the corner beckoned irresistibly. After weeks of walking, endless nights of sleeping on the bare ground or mats, the temptation was too great.

"False alarm," Chick concluded, and tumbled into bed.

At dawn he was awakened by a pounding on the door below. Apparently the Ozamis family had returned without their keys. Sleepily Chick yawned, sighed, and reached for his shorts. Halfway down the stairs, on the landing, something prompted him to look out the window above the front door.

At the curb sat a Jap truck. The men hammering on the door were quite definitely sons of the Emperor. Once too often Chick had listened to the cry of "Wolf!"

Frantically dashing back to his bedroom, Chick bundled up his papers. Documents, maps, reports, letters from guerrilla chieftains to General MacArthur, containing figures and statistics—in the hands of the enemy this material would spell disaster, not only to Chick personally but to the whole guerrilla movement. It simply could not be lost.

Chick wasted little time cursing his own carelessness, but made furious mental reconnaissance of the house. As was customary in many small towns in the Philippines, the lower floor was devoted to drugstore and warehouse, the upper to living quarters. All windows, below and above, were iron-barred.

There was an opening into the attic, but too high to be reached without placing a couple of chairs on a table. And how to dispose of the chairs, once he had gained this dubious sanctuary?

Chick discarded this possibility at once. The only remaining outlet was in the kitchen, from which back stairs led to a door facing the side street.

If the Japanese have come into the back yard, Chick thought, I'm a plucked duck.

Below, the front door began to shatter.

Clad only in shorts, moccasin slippers, and Navy cap, and clutching his bundle of verbal dynamite, Chick slipped down the rear stairs. Peeking around the sill, he saw that the Japs were devoting all their attention and energies to the front door. To the back fence was only a matter of a few feet. Beyond lay coconut groves, the hills, and safety.... Chick braced himself.

Normally I should have had some difficulty in placing a hand on the top of tins fence and vaulting it. As it was I do not remember touching the top at all as I sailed over. Now and then fear is a great ally.

Not until he got to the sanctuary of the hills did Chick begin to breathe easier. Friends and townspeople crowded around him, expressing great emotion and relief, for it was felt sure that he had been captured.

"I would have said a mass for your soul, Chico," said Father Calanan, the tall young Irish padre of the town, "only for the fact that in the sudden arrival of the Japanese and the haste of my departure I was forced to leave all the holy vessels in the church."

Chick's face grew thoughtful.

"The can of wheat flour for Communion wafers. Padre?"

"Alas, that too," said the priest sadly. "Even as you appeared just now I was considering a return to recover these treasures."

"Bueno!" Chick decided. "I will go with you."

It is difficult, perhaps, for one who is neither Catholic nor Filipino to understand just what this can of Communion flour—which Chick had brought all the way from Australia—meant to the devout priest, and would mean to multitudes of the people.

With the war, as Chick had occasion to observe throughout the countryside, increasing numbers of Filipinos wished to take Communion. The supply of consecrated wine had fallen so low that the priests were reduced to administering it with a medicine dropper. Wheat flour, normally an import, was completely missing. This fifty-pound can, which Chick had been inspired to include with his supplies at the last moment, was the first to be seen on Mindanao in almost two years.

It was. Chick realized, a morale-building item of the highest importance to an extremely religious people. No more effective proof that the aid really was coming could have been brought in at this time than the material for the true wafers of the Church.

Delivering his vital documents into trusted guerrilla hands, with explicit instructions as to their delivery to Colonel Fertig should he not return. Commander Parsons now set out with Father Calanan.

Cautiously they made their way back down the trail over which Chick had so recently panted. The church was on a knoll overlooking the entire city. Below them, as they reconnoitered from the protection of the jungle, they could see intense enemy activity. On the shore troops and supplies were being landed in quantity.

This, Chick immediately saw, was no mere routine landing of a patrol from a couple of launches. It was rather a definite movement of the Japanese against Colonel Fertig's guerrilla forces, a tangible recognition of guerrilla power by the enemy.

"The Japs are in the body of the town. Father," Chick murmured. "I don't think they've climbed up as far as the church yet. Let me just slip down ..."

The priest smiled and shook his head. He was a worthy representative of his order and of the Philippine padres who had done and were to do so much to uphold the spirit of their people and aid the free movement—even to the sacrifice of life itself.

"This duty belongs to me," said Father Calanan.

"To both of us, then," Chick added gently. "I brought the flour in for the Filipino people, not for the Japanese."

Darting across the clearing, they gained the dim, cool confines of the church without interference. Before the altar the priest calmly went through his accustomed obeisance. Then he gathered up the sacred utensils and the altar cloth, while Chick tucked the can of wheat flour under his arm.

"Anything else, Padre?" he inquired.

Father Calanan disappeared into the vestry, from which he presently staggered with his arms full of religious costumes ordinarily used for festivals of the Church.

"I do not know how long we shall have to remain in the hills," he explained. "Many of my little ones are already naked. The Blessed Mary will not object if we divert the purpose of these garments to cover the little children."

"But how," Chick objected, "are we going to carry these burdens up the steep trail?"

The father smiled.

"There are two ponies in the stables." Filipino ponies are about the size of Shetlands, but capable of carrying their own weight.

On these small animals the priest and the former polo-playing stevedore rode safely back into the hills.

I could never do enough for the priests of the Philippines. Not because I am a Catholic—but because they are men.

This particular invasion of the Japanese, Chick quickly learned, was made in a force numbering possibly four thousand men. The area in which he now found himself was intensely patrolled and occupied, even to the mountains. The Japanese had wearied of urging Colonel Fertig and his unsurrendered soldiers to come in and give themselves up. Now they had decided on a different type of "propaganda."

Their efforts, as usual, left them baffled and bruised.

Endeavoring to make his way through the Jap lines to reach Fertig's mobile headquarters, Chick had many opportunities for firsthand observance of guerrilla warfare at its best and most effective.

The usual process, he found, was for the Japs to arrive in an area with mortars, machine guns, a good supply of ammunition, and set up in deployment on the theory that the guerrillas would come out and fight. Their optimism was boundless, previous experience to the contrary, and they would plug away for four or five hours.

The guerrillas would answer with just enough fire to keep the enemy hopeful that they would make a charge.

Meanwhile every minute of delay was scoring on the guerrilla side. Not only did it permit the civilians to get out and up into the hills, but it allowed the main guerrilla force to deploy in the region through which the Japs must come on their inward march.

Guerrilla warfare, Chick came to understand, thus means purely defensive-offensive tactics. Defensive in the beginning when the Japs arrive, and the guerrillas move into previously prepared positions; offensive in that, as soon as the enemy stops to rest or comes up into the mountains in single file along the trails, ambush is employed, and the guerrilla rifle comes into prominent offensive action.

Fertig's erratic movements—and he was to be on the move for the greater part of the next year and a half, not only to save his own neck but to avoid pressure on the people in whose areas he had found it convenient to stay—now kept Commander Parsons playing a game of hide-and-seek with the Japs for several days.

It also taught him a number of valuable lessons, which he had to learn the hard way.

The shortage of clothing applied to guerrillas, of course, as well as civilians. Hence the jungle fighters made it a practice to strip their fallen enemies and wear Jap uniforms in their daily activities. The average guerrilla soldier is a youngster, seventeen to twenty-three years old, standing five feet two to six, weighing from a hundred and ten to a hundred and twenty pounds. This similarity of physical stature and uniform thus made it extremely difficult, from afar, to distinguish friend from foe.

Commander Parsons did not forget the first lesson in recognition learned upon the beach in his original landing. The Japanese, due to superstition, never goes barefooted—and Chick in recognition it a rule to look first at the feet of a group approaching along a trail.

Another clue to the identity of strangers was the presence in the party of anyone not wearing a Jap uniform. If six wore uniforms and the seventh did not, Chick could be fairly certain he was about to meet friends.

The best bet, Commander Parsons now found as he dodged along the trails of Mindanao, was to have a guide walk ahead and warn of the approach of the enemy. The guide, passing as an innocent farmer, would be unmolested by the Japs. Chick would dive into the brush.

When in doubt, I always dove anyway.

In this manner, scratched and weary—but with his documentary evidence of guerrilla strength and loyalty intact—Chick finally reached the headquarters of Colonel Fertig, where he was greeted with considerable relief and joy.

"Chico, my boy," said the tall colonel, "we knew you had been cut off and we thought you were captured. In fact I have so advised the headquarters of General MacArthur."

Chick sat down on the steps of Colonel Fertig's temporary office and began to pick thorns out of his arms and legs with the only weapon he ever carried, a nail file.

"I was certainly cut off and I dam near got caught," he confessed. "Anyway, here I am. Is Charlie Smith here?"

Smith, who made the original landing with Chick, had been busy installing coast-watcher radio stations at strategic points chosen by the commander and Colonel Fertig. He was still part of the party.

"Present and accounted for," said the colonel. "Charlie's done a grand job. But we're going to need trained personnel to man these stations if your program really goes through.

Our former Philippine Telegraph Company employees and the 'sparks' from the American groups are pretty well-placed right now."

"The program is going through," said Chick with conviction, "and you'll get your men. Colonel Courtney Whitney has recruited volunteers from the Filipino regiments back in the States. They're in training at a special school in Australia right now. I'll bring you a batch next time I come."

"Fine," said Colonel Fertig. "I've got three passengers for your return trip, American officers who just escaped from the Davao Penal Colony. General MacArthur wants you to bring them out."

"Are they in condition to walk? It looks as though we'd have a bit of a hike cross-country to the coast."

"They should be able to make it. I've been feeding them up while you played tag with the Nips. Oh yes," the colonel added, elaborately casual. "Old friend of yours turned up the other day. Imagine you'll be kind of glad to see him." He turned his head toward his office. "You can come out now, Captain."

A slight, wiry young man in faded American officer's uniform stepped out on the porch. "Hello, Chico," he said, and grinned.

"Tommy Jurika," Chick breathed, as though seeing a ghost.

"Poor relations are always popping up at odd times, eh?" said Chick's brother-in-law.

The two men embraced warmly, for Tommy—a captain in the USAFFE forces in Cebu at the time of surrender—had been thought captured by the Japanese.

Tommy admitted wryly, "The good colonel here tells me you're the original male Mata Hari."

"Artful Dodger, is more like it," smiled Chick. "You ought to see my swan dive from a low trail into a thorn-bush."

"I'll bet that's something. How're Katsy and the three muchachitos?"

"Fine, last I heard."

Tommy hesitated. "And Mother Jurika?" he asked haltingly. "I hear she wouldn't go with you and the family."

Chick shook his head. "She stuck around. . . ."

"Because of me," said Tommy. "Oh, I know. I guess," he added slowly, "that's my next destination—Manila."

Chick paused. Tommy Jurika was only twenty-eight. Yet he knew the Islands and the guerrillas better, even, than Chick did.

"Listen, Tommy," he began thoughtfully. "I've got a bigger job for you than that, even, because it affects more people. If I promise to do everything possible to get Madre Jurika out of Manila, will you help me?"

Tommy raised his eyes. "Help you do what—fight the Japs?"

"It's not as spectacular as that," Chick said. "But it's more important in the long run: supplying the guys who fight the Japs. I want you on my staff, Tommy."

"Where would I operate?"

"At the advance bases of Spyron subs. I'd like to bring you out next time I go."

"And Mother Jurika?" Tommy returned to the original subject. "It's not going to be healthy to be the mother-in-law of Chick Parsons, in Manila, pretty soon."

"I know that. But I've got an idea. . ."

Tommy smiled. "If you've got an idea, it's as good as done. Okay, I'll think it over."

"Good," said Chick. They shook hands, wordlessly.

A radio operator stepped out of his shack nearby and saluted.

"We are in contact with General MacArthur's headquarters. Colonel," he said.

The colonel looked at Chick.

"Roger," said Commander Parsons. "I'll punch this one out myself and get one of those salt-water taxis headed in this direction. I want to toss these papers on the chief's desk before they burn me up completely. I'm pretty badly scorched, as is."

Chick Parsons strode off to order a submarine.

CHAPTER VII

WHILE NOT IN THE BEST OF PHYSICAL CONDITION, I did not antici-
pate anything more than a sturdy walk in reaching the submarine
rendezvous.

In time, the Japanese would come to want Commander Parsons as
badly—if not more so—than they wanted Colonel Fertig. Right now, July 1,
1943, Parsons was only a name on the books of the Kempeitai, a United States
naval officer who had pulled a fast one in getting himself and his family out
of Manila the year before. The Japs could not conceive of anyone but a mad-
man coming back for a second try. They did not yet know the American
temperament very well.

But Wendell W. Fertig, acknowledged leader of the guerrilla forces on
Mindanao, was another proposition. His capture and the destruction of his
forces was the chief objective of the punitive force of four thousand yellow as-
sassins now scouring Mindanao.

The colonel had therefore found it necessary to establish mountain headquarters in the northern hills of Occidental Misamis. Here he took full
advantage of the new equipment Commander Parsons had brought him to
direct the harassing of his pursuers through the radio network of his guerrilla
soldiers.

Since Fertig's general whereabouts was never very much or very long in
doubt to the Japanese, Chick decided that the southern part of Mindanao
might be found relatively free of the panting patrols of the enemy. An exchange of radio messages with General MacArthur's headquarters, therefore,
decided on a lonely bay on the south coast as point of contact by United
States submarine.

Chick's party consisted of a small bunch of guerrilla commandos, to act
as guides and bearers, Charlie Smith, and the three ex-prisoners of war. This
trio, whose story is well-known in the United States, included Lieutenant Commander Melvin H. McCoy, survivor of a gallant United States destroyer;
Colonel Stephen Melnick, former Intelligence officer; and Lieutenant Colonel
William E. Dyess, onetime member of General MacArthur's staff on Bataan. It
was Dyess' hard fate to survive the most arduous of confinements and hair-
raising of escapes, which he later chronicled in book form, only to be killed in
a plane crash in the United States.

One tommy gun and two pistols with a limited amount of ammunition
was the only protection the group had. Their most important item was Chick's
briefcase, containing the invaluable Intelligence material destined to be the
basis for the entire project of supplying the peculiar needs of the guerrillas.

The bay was a good five days' hike, Chick figured, from Colonel Fertig's present HQ. He added another day for good measure.

Just how optimistic this was will now be related, without quotes or comment, by Lieutenant Commander Charles Parsons under the title "A Sturdy Walk across Mindanao."

We planned to reach the first day's destination by 3 or 4 P.M. at the latest. Encountered no difficulty until midday.

At this point we came upon a bridge over a deep, crocodile-infested stream, which was still burning. Since we felt sure there were no Japs in the region, we decided it was the work of guerrillas.

Enough timbers remained for the manufacture of a raft, so while two members stood by with guns watching for crocs the rest of the party turned to and constructed a raft. This unexpected barrier held up our schedule so that we did not succeed in reaching the first barrio, or native village, where we figured the locals would have enough food to feed us, until after five o'clock.

We were very tired and slogged along, heads down, paying little attention to what was ahead. Presently we came close enough to make out the first native house—when Colonel Dyess let out a yell. A number of Japanese were taking a bath in the yard!

The Japs discovered us at the same time and dashed for their clothes and arms—while we made a hasty retreat to the mountain nearby.

It was dark and raining as we started up the mountain. The trail was muddy and slippery. We dared not shine a light and had to feel our way, slipping and sliding and making little progress. It was felt certain that the Japs were right behind us and we could not stop for a moment's rest. We had had nothing to eat all day and felt rather sorry for ourselves as we had looked forward to a comfortable meal and rest with friends in this particular town.

After four or five hours of the most exhausting kind of climbing we reached a clearing near the top of the mountain, where we found a cornfield, always an indication that a house is near. We were so hungry that as we went through the field we pulled off raw ears and crammed them into our mouths. They tasted more delicious than ice-cream sodas.

Beyond the field was a small native bamboo hut, fifteen feet square, into which was jammed almost the entire population of townspeople. These people told us that a Jap patrol, numbering about fifty, had entered their town below early that morning, and that they had barely succeeded in getting out. They were most hospitable and, though without much below early us two or three chickens. These were barbecued and eaten without much attention to bones, feathers, or anything else.

Dyess, McCoy, and Melnick decided to try and wedge in among the two score or more people in the house, for the night. Charlie Smith, however, had discovered a chicken house, perhaps seven feet square, nearby, and thought it a good place to stay if we could get rid of the chickens. I saw no particular difficulty in doing this. We shooed the hens out into the night, cleaned the place out, laid down Dyess' shelter half, and pulled our one blanket over us. We felt rather pleased with ourselves as we dropped off to sleep.

However, we reckoned without the chickens, who returned in the night. When we awakened at four o'clock in the morning, to get an early start, we found chickens all over us. Four or five hens and a couple of roosters were perched on me and a like number on Charlie. It seemed that every one of them had dysentery!

This embarrassing little matter was rectified in a nearby stream. The hospitable people in the hut provided corn and more barbecued chicken for breakfast and loaned us a guide who claimed he could show us a short cut over the mountain to the trail which should easily lead us to our second day's destination. We set out, therefore, and all morning stumbled down the mountain trail, of which the guide seemed to know far less than we did. We were constantly lost, in fact we were never anything else but lost. Charlie Smith finally took over, having the only compass in the party, and guided us down streams and through spring beds, anywhere we could go without having to cut our way through thick jungle.

Considerably later than expected, we struck the trail. Time was precious, and we were quite concerned over the delay but, once on the trail, our spirits mounted. We went along, cheerful and whistling, for half an hour. Suddenly Smith, who was up in front with me, glanced down—and stopped short. In the soft mud were imprints of rubber soles with the tabby, or one-toed design, which is used by only one soldier in the world—the Jap.

Very forcefully, then, it was brought to our attention that the Japs had split their patrol, half coming around the mountain, half going over it—after us. In fact they had actually passed us as we were scrambling around taking our short cut. We were now chasing the Japs who had been sent out to get us!

There was only one trail and nothing to do but march on, taking what precautions against ambush we could. We stripped a couple of commando lads down, so they would look exactly like the people of the country and sent them on ahead to warn us if they came on the Jap patrol or a trap. Around three that afternoon we found ourselves so close to the enemy as to spot cigarette butts, still burning, along the trail.

It was amusing to see a commando lad pick up a butt, take a couple of puffs, and throw it away, with the remark: "I don't like it. It's Jap, not American."

Shortly thereafter we were going along an open space at the top of a rise when out from the grass popped an old Moro woman. We could not understand what she said but her gestures were eloquent enough. She apparently had been asked by the Japs if any Americans were on the trail and, putting two and two together, had popped out from the goodness of her heart to warn us that the enemy was just over the hill.

In fact, reconnaissance proved that they were taking it easy in a coconut grove at the foot of our rise, washing their rations down with coconut milk.

Our appreciation for what the old Moro woman did cannot be expressed in words alone. There was no rhyme nor reason for her warning us, except friendship for everyone but the Japanese.

We had had no food since morning, the Japs having cleaned out the two or three villages we had encountered.

The thought—and sight—of the enemy filling his stomach while ours were empty was almost more than we could bear. Charlie Smith was all for trying to eliminate the men in the grove, but soberer consideration proved that even if each bullet found its mark we would not have enough ammunition to take care of half the patrol. Besides, our mission was much more important than the pleasure, as Smith considered it, of knocking off a few Japs.

The trail divided at the grove below and, munching on leaves to stay our hunger, we sat with fingers crossed, waiting to see which direction the Japanese would take. If they took the left trail we were safe, as ours led straight ahead. If they continued on we would have to do likewise, for we had no other course.

Luck was with us. The Japs took the left trail. As soon as they were out of sight we proceeded on our way straight ahead, our morale high despite the lack of food. We really did knots before nightfall and got well away from them. We later learned that the Japs, after going down the left trail for a while, backtracked and started chasing us again. We had such a good lead that it would have been very difficult for them to have caught us anyway. We were far more concerned with the fact that we had already wasted one day, going over the mountain, and must do full time in order to make our rendezvous.

We had no possible manner of getting word ahead nor had we radio communications to ask the submarine to wait—and missing our rendezvous would be very serious indeed. Not only were Melnick, McCoy, and Dyess very anxious to get out—General MacArthur was most eager to have the latest information from them regarding atrocities committed against prisoners of war. Smith and I had been almost six months in the country and the information we had collected and the observations we had made were likewise anxiously awaited by GHQ. If we did not make this rendezvous there was considerable doubt that we would be able to make another in the near future, due to increased activity in this area ahead. In fact, so much pressure was being exerted on Colonel Fertig, we later learned, that he had increased activity stern Mindanao and go into the eastern portion to prevent damage to his organization.

All of these elements—some of which we knew, others merely suspected—kept us going at a smart pace despite our hunger and fatigue. About dusk, we came upon a recently evacuated house where Colonel Dyess managed to run down a chicken. This fowl, with some green papayas, camotes, or sweet potatoes, and corn enabled us to piece together a meal which was entirely inadequate for the amount of physical work we were doing. Then we pressed on in the darkness as the only sure way of outdistancing the Japanese, who, by reason of regular rations and the fact that they were following a clear trail while we were frequently lost, we figured could walk as far if not farther and faster than we could.

The third day found us fighting our way up and down the most difficult mountain trails I have ever encountered. Very slightly used even in peacetime, they consisted in spots of mud into which we sank to the knees. Our feet were constantly wet, and five minutes of every hour were devoted to the taking off of shoes and removal of gravel—for while I went barefooted most of the time, the rest of the men wore GI shoes. From morning till night we were wringing wet from rain, perspiration, and the streams we had to wade. When wading was impossible a raft had to be built to ferry across our perishable equipment—especially my brief case with its precious documents.

Even when we came out into the open the heat was terrific, and water was a problem as McCoy had the only canteen among us. He went through the motions of purifying the water with halazone tablets, but since the natives have drunk from the streams for years without ill effects we finally yielded to this necessity. Since we never found enough food to carry an emergency ration you can imagine our relief, the third night, on coming upon a barn containing two cows and four goats.

This emotion, however, was of short duration. On discarding the slaughter of the cow as too much of a good thing, we found that the goats made such a human bleating that no one wished to kill them. This dilemma was happily solved by the return of one of our commandos with the welcome news that he had found people half a mile away who would kill a pig and cook some corn rice for us.

A detail went off and shortly returned with arms full of food. They bore, wrapped in banana leaves, a huge feast of barbecued pork. This, plus corn ground down to the size of hominy grits and steamed like rice, provided us with the finest meal of our lives. It was just like sitting at the Waldorf-Astoria in New York City with thirty waiters bringing on course after course.

We rolled into our blankets in the loft of the barn, thankful that we had not been force waiters bringing or goat. The latter were very vociferous in their gratitude, during the night, but that didn't bother anyone. And while we slept, our guerrilla lads, despite their weariness, stood guard.

These boys were fine upstanding men who had gone through a commando course in Colonel Fertig's school and graduated with high honors. This course was a premium and reward for gone through bravery in actual fire against the Japanese, and on our journey across Mindanao the boys were worth their weight in gold.

The morning of the fourth day we arose at four o'clock, as usual, warmed over and ate the remnant of our feast of the night before, and prepared to press on. Our ranks were swelled by the arrival of four or five soldiers who had evacuated from Aurora, a town near our original first day's destination; they claimed that the patrol was not too far behind us. The addition of these men and their rifles boosted our morale but caused our party to be that much more conspicuous, as well as providing more mouths to feed. Nevertheless we were glad to have their company.

At this point we felt that the situation was well in hand and were in fact most hopeful of making our rendezvous on schedule—when we ran across the worst river we had yet encountered. Deep, swift-moving, and difficult to swim, this river necessitated the building of another bamboo raft. There was slight compensation, however, in the fact that the sole remaining member of a nearby village possessed a lot of chickens and a very complete supply of food. A most hospitable individual, this man not only provided food but cooked us a marvelous feast.

Thus fortified, we made our way half a mile upstream and set to work on the raft. Learning that there was a guerrilla camp ahead of us, and hopeful that we might find radio facilities to warn the submarine of our possible delay, Dyess and I went on ahead. While the others were making the raft we took off our trousers, tied the legs and inflated them, in a manner familiar to every GI. On these makeshift water wings we kicked our way across the river.

We also had with us on this advance mission for food and preparation a guide. We walked for two hours, not backtracking once—only to bring up short exactly where we had started. In fact we arrived just in time to meet our friends coming across on the raft! To weary men who had walked all day this was most heartbreaking. But to excuse the guide, it must be pointed out that these trails are so little used that even the guides have only a small knowledge of them.

This time Charlie Smith and his compass kept us fairly well in the right direction. For some reason Commander McCoy, who had been showing signs of strain, took the guide and went ahead. As darkness came on we lost contact with him entirely. We failed to make the guerrilla encampment that afternoon but spent the night in a small village where we obtained sufficient food from the two remaining inhabitants to sustain us. By noon of the following day, the fifth of our journey, we came upon the guerrilla camp.

Captain Medina—now Major Medina—was in charge of the guerrilla forces in this area and we were very happy indeed to see him. Our worry about Commander McCoy was relieved by finding that he had preceded us to the village. He gave a very hazy explanation of his actions in going on ahead with the guide and we realized that he was badly in need of medical care—further necessity for making our rendezvous on time.

Captain Medina, immediately on learning of our Jap pursuers, sent out a detachment to ambush and delay the patrol. Later we learned that the Japs had been driven back with the loss of ten or twelve of their men—which brought reprisal the patrol Medina and forced him up into the hills. On our next visit to Mindanao, a few months later, we would be forced to skirt enemy territory in this region and would not be able to go along well-known trails.

At this time, however, everything was okay in the area. We spent half a day with Medina, putting away a lot of good chow, trying to persuade McCoy to rest, and generally getting set for our final lap.

We thought, then, that we were well on schedule.

Incidentally, while we were there a spy was brought into camp and given a guerrilla trial. This man was a Filipino who had been brought over from Cotabato by the Japanese and sent behind guerrilla lines.

Testimony was recorded in due form and affidavit. The spy stated why he was behind the lines and for what purpose he had been hired by the Japanese. He revealed what information he had secured and also admitted that he had been working as a mechanic on a Jap launch and had, in fact, been supplying the enemy with regular information of guerrilla strength and movements.

At the conclusion of testimony the spy was pronounced guilty and immediately executed with a Moro-type barong, or sword. Colonel Dyess thought the sword would be a suitable souvenir for his father, and the sergeant who performed the execution agreeably presented it to him. We left immediately after witnessing this bit of guerrilla justice and spent the night in a deserted schoolhouse. I had often slumbered on a school bench before, but for pleasure and not by necessity.

Thus we came to our sixth day, the day we were to make rendezvous with the sub. To our intense concern, the guide's sense of direction deserted him entirely and we lost our way completely during the morning. Wandering hopelessly from place to place, we found no habitation or people. On every hill we expected to glimpse the blue waters of the bay but rise followed rise and nothing, but jungle stretched before us. All we knew was that we were going in the correct westerly direction according to Smith's compass.

We kept plugging along at any trail we could see, wondering if we had suffered all these hardships and come this long way only to fail when our mission was so nearly complete.

About four o'clock, to our intense joy, we did see the bay and ran into a small village which somebody recognized as being about two miles from destination. Stopping only long enough to drink a coconut apiece, we pressed on over the last two miles, the hardest two miles I have ever traveled. At destination we found Captain McCarthy with a launch waiting for us.

Captain McCarthy was in charge of guerrilla groups in that particular area and had been waiting for two days. Colonel Fertig had sent him information that we were coming, indicating that we might be delayed. This information McCarthy had relayed to the submarine, but whether or not it had been received he did not know. He now took us across to his place in the launch and sent out another message, indicating that we had arrived. Inasmuch as there were Japanese patrols and launches in the area, the rendezvous point was also changed.

We spent the night with Captain McCarthy and it seemed grand to be in what you might call civilization again. The next morning we turned over to him everything we had left including clothing, money, arms, and ammunition as we expected to pick up everything we should need on board the sub.

Not daring to go down to our rendezvous openly in the launch, we went to great trouble to camouflage the vessel with coconut fronds and other vegetation until we actually resembled a floating island. Hugging the shore, we went from McCarthy's place to an island, where we remained hidden until about four. Now came the most ticklish part of the whole business, as we had to navigate about four or five miles to the east and right out into the middle of the bay to reach our rendezvous spot.

We had agreed on certain signals which would indicate to the sub on submerged reconnaissance that everything was okay. On reaching the rendezvous point, these signals were raised and for two hours we sat.

Many of us thought it extremely problematical that the submarine would surface. There was, as indicated, no evidence that word of our delayed arrival had reached the sub. Nor had the skipper given any sign that he had received information regarding the change of rendezvous. The long strain under which the prisoners of war had been, plus the latest and immediate strain of having been chased by the enemy for several days, all rendered us extremely anxious.

Charlie Smith, my companion on this and many other expeditions, is a cold-blooded, unemotional "sourpuss." I have never seen him smile, much less laugh. Just at sunset he grabbed me around the neck and let out what would almost be a scream.

"There it is!" he shouted.

The reaction of the others was very marked. One burst into tears. Another sat down and stared. The third joined Smith and me with arms about each other in silent witness of what seemed to us to be a miracle.

Actually it was but the routine surfacing of a submarine.

PART II

THE AID

CHAPTER VIII

I BECAME THE MESSENGER BOY BETWEEN THOSE TWO splendid gentlemen, Colonel Courtney Whitney of the Army and Captain A. H. McCollum of the Navy, whose tolerance for my antics and eccentricities of movement made it possible to do this work successfully.

Reporting back to General MacArthur in Australia, Chick Parsons summed up for the general's staff all he had learned in his secret survey of the Philippines.

War brings new phrases to the lips of a people. Out of their misery and distress, their hope and despair, a word alien to the mother tongue now and again creeps into the language and remains there, symbolizing the universal longing of an oppressed people.

Such a phrase, in the Philippine Islands prior to invasion, was "the Aid." Everywhere Commander Parsons went on his first mission to the Islands the burning question of the hour was, "When will the Aid come?"

To be sure, the question had the immediate meaning—

"When will General MacArthur return and kick out the Japs?" But to the Filipino people the phrase had far deeper connotations. The Aid meant the return to a way of life and thought and action which the people had never fully appreciated, perhaps, until it was lost to them.

Just how very much the Filipino people had lost no one knew better than Chick Parsons.

Wandering through big and little towns, up mountain trails and across open farm country. Chick talked with hundreds of people. Neither puppets nor guerrillas, these be wilder mountain trails war carried on at the only tasks they knew because it was necessary, for some reason, to keep on living. Not daring to resist the Japanese because their wives and children would suffer. Afraid to speak aloud the phrase which echoed with each beat of their hearts. "The Aid ... "The Aid ..."

Crouching in the guerrilla-held hills of Mindanao and Leyte at night. Chick tuned in the Jap-controlled broadcasts from Manila or Cebu, and listened to the Japanese Propaganda Corps labor to effect the friendly co-operation of the Philippine people with Japan. To these honeyed phrases-out of what he knew, what he had seen, and what he had learned—Chick made his own responses.

"We have freed your brave Filipino soldiers, even those taken prisoner on Bataan," said the voice of Co-Prosperity." We have granted amnesty to countless others. . . ."

Those few who would come in, thought Chick, glancing at the faces of the listening guerrillas, mindful of the thousands waiting in the darkness all over the Islands.

"We have continued in office your trusted public servants. ..."

The puppets will be taken care of by the guerrillas, the secretly loyal the free movement will use.

"We have given to those of you who have already recognized the benign light of the Rising Sun independence, freedom, liberty—such as you never enjoyed beneath the crushing exploitation of the United States. . .

Liberty—to join a Japanese Neighborhood Society, or starve; to listen only to Jap broadcasts, read Jap newspapers, attend Jap movies. Freedom—to hang by the wrists until dead, for striking back at a brutal sentry, for failing to bow three times to a Jap officer. The hundred and one cruelties Chick had seen visited on the people of the occupied sections by the Kempeitai rushed through his mind, as they rushed through the minds of millions of Filipinos, sternly canceling the promises of the propagandists. Independence? Only here in the hills did it exist, unceasing vigilance its price.

"Many of your fellow men are living in far greater luxury and comfort than ever before. They have automobiles, money . . ."

In Manila alone. Chick knew, thousands of automobiles had been seized, stripped, pressed, baled, and shipped to Japan as scrap. In the rural districts tons of mechanical and farm equipment, the lifeblood of an agricultural country, had suffered a similar fate. All the nickel and copper coins had been gathered in, sent to Japan to be melted down into bombs and bullets and planes—and hurled back at guerrilla soldier and civilian Filipino alike. Oh, the people had money. Some of them, that is. Japanese invasion currency. Worthless script.

"Japan has brought health and happiness to the liberated people of the Philippines ..."

Malaria, pellagra, beriberi, typhus . . . everywhere hundreds dying.

"Your United States has deserted you. Your MacArthur has fled, leaving only a vague phrase to haunt you. He will never return. Japan is your friend. Japan . . .

Chick snapped off the radio. Waited . . . for the inevitable question. Out of the night, in the soft patient voice of the Filipino, it came.

"Commander, cuando vendra the Aid?"

Reporting back to General MacArthur in the late summer of 1943, after almost six months in the Islands, Commander Parsons brought much more than definite assurance of a strong resistance movement throughout the Philippines. He was able to paint a picture of a people completely fed-up with the Japanese, bitterly disillusioned, acutely aware that in place of a pleasant, democratic way of life they had gained only misery, hunger, and poverty, both spiritual and physical. A people who wanted only one Co-Prosperity Sphere—and that with the United States.

Chick started to accumulate personnel for what later turned out to be Spyron—as Parsons' force, handling a group of subs specifically set aside for special missions, was affectionately and unofficially known.

Upon his arrival in the Southwest Pacific Area, Colonel Whitney was placed at the head of the Philippine Regional Section and given the job of setting up an organization charged with the responsibility of arming every guerrilla-soldier before D-Day of the invasion. Parsons was in the Islands when Colonel Whitney arrived and took over, but he had known Courtney several years ago, and it did not take long for the two to get together in working out plans for arming the guerrillas. Colonel Whitney was the boss, rant he administrative end of the outfit, and Parsons was the operational member, doing the messenger work—the outside man, as it were.

As the best man available to secure from Army and civilian sources the equipment needed by the guerrillas. Chick had tabbed Tommy Jurika, his brother-in-law. He summoned Tommy by submarine, appointing Captain George Kinsler of the Army to assist him. From the Navy, Chick borrowed Ensign William Hagans, Philippine born and raised, and placed him in charge of forward bases where submarines fuel and load. At semi forward bases he located Lieutenant Lee Strickland of the Navy, whom he described as "adventuresome, full of pep, a real Spyron guerrilla."

Thereupon Spyron rolled up its sleeves.

It was a novel arrangement to have Army officers working at Navy bases and vice versa, and we were looked upon as mystery men. The hush-hush nature of our business, prior to invasion, made it necessary to order supplies without indicating purpose or destination. If word of what we were up to got out to the enemy, it meant our necks. . . .

So far as numbers were concerned, Spyron was an insignificant organization. But behind it were the great supply lines of the United States Army, the mighty underwater fleet of the Navy.

And Chick Parsons? Right in the middle.

Chick also occupied a similar position in the Seventh Fleet, of which Captain A. H. McCollum was the staff officer in charge of Navy affairs where the guerrillas of the Philippines were concerned. Chick's most immediate Navy contact was with Captain McCollum; he also worked closely with Commodore Fife, the original commander of Task Force 72, and later with Commodore Jack Haines, who relieved Jimmie Fife about the time that Spyron got going full speed.

On neither staff did he have any command function.

Chick, then, was like a skipper without a ship, a battalion commander without a battalion, free to come and go at will.

"I was the errand boy," he said.

In the fall of '43 and winter of '44, the theater of war in New Guinea had enormous demands to make. The equipment the guerrillas needed was in many instances of a very special nature. Consequently the "errands" took some running, and here Chick found an invaluable friend and ally in Colonel Whitney.

A former Air Corps pilot, Courtney Whitney had taken up the study of law in Manila, passed the bar exams, established a brilliant practice, and made a fortune in mining on the side. He loved the Philippines and its people as did Chick, and when war came it was inevitable that he should be drawn to MacArthur's staff.

Colonel Whitney was thoroughly in approval of the guerrilla movement and its aims. He had personally picked six hundred volunteers from the Filipino regiments in the States and helped establish a school in Australia, known as Tabragalba, for the training of these men as guerrilla specialists—radio coast watchers, weather and plane observers, saboteurs, booby-trap experts, and artillerymen.

Armed with the highest and most unquestioned of priorities, secured in many cases directly from General MacArthur, Colonel Whitney proceeded to devote all his energies to securing the stuff needed for the guerrillas.

Signal equipment, powerful enough to reach Australia, light enough to be transported quickly in an emergency. Small copper stills for the extraction of alcohol from the coconut palm and the gabi root. Hundreds of carbines— the weapon whose lightness and rapid-fire power had been found ideal for the jungle fighters. Ammunition and spare parts for both new guerrilla weapons and their old ones—the Enfields, Springfields, Jap rifles, and paltiks.

"Now what in hell is a paltik?" inquired the colonel when Chick first confronted him with the word.

"The paltik," Chick explained with a smile, "is a home-made shotgun. You take a wooden stock, chisel out a groove, and fit into it a water pipe, reinforced at one end by copper wire or adhesive tape. Sink a nail at the base of the groove with the point out. Insert a shotgun shell into the pipe. Aim the thing in the general direction of a Jap—and pull the pipe back against the nail. Simple!"

The colonel threw up his hands. "Sounds a lot more dangerous to the user than to the enemy."

"Oh, sometimes it backfires, but by and large the paltik is more effective than you might think. Many of the guerrillas swear by it."

"Shotgun shells loaded with Double-O pellets for the paltiks. Bolts, triggers, hammers to replace worn-out parts on outmoded rifles." Colonel Whitney sighed. "I'll be glad when you've weaned your guerrillas to the carbine and tommy gun, Chick."

"So will I," Chick agreed. "I'm hoping that every guerrilla will have his own weapon, and a good one, by the time General MacArthur climbs down the landing nets."

"A large order," said Colonel Whitney. "Now about the medicines . . ."

"An absolute must. Triple A priority," said Chick, thinking of the terrible physical conditions he had observed and the heartbreaking efforts of the guerrillas to combat such diseases as malaria.

Sometime before the war Colonel Arthur Fisher, director of forestry, had brought into the Islands seedlings of the cinchona, a South American tree whose bark contains quinine crystals. A site was selected in the Del Monte region of Mindanao, west of Malaybalay, and a plantation started. By wartime there were eleven million trees on the plantation and the Army had set up a plant nearby to extract the quinine.

Lacking imports of sulphuric acid, necessary to jar the quinine loose from the bark, the plant closed down. The guerrillas, however, kept up the plantation, and Chick had found them desperately endeavoring to extract the drug by most primitive methods—boiling the bark into a brew or grinding it up into powder and mixing it with corn flour into a pasty pill.

"How did these methods work out?" the colonel inquired.

"They didn't. The liquid was too weak to be effective. Patients shortly became allergic to the paste pills and unable to stomach any more of the mess. Five hundred persons a day are dying of malaria on Mindanao alone."

Colonel Whitney wrote "atabrine" and "quinine," underscoring the words three times. Serums and vitamin tablets were also added to the list.

"Anything else for your first trip?" Colonel Whitney inquired.

Chick consulted the shorthand notes he had jotted down.

"I'd like to take in a few personal items for the chiefs. Real stuff they can't get."

In guerrilla parlance Chick had found two English words in constant use, referring to articles of daily welfare. "Real"—pronounced "re-al"—meant imported or prewar. "Emergency"—accent on the e—substitute.

"Pendatun," Chick continued, "has a very snappy cavalry outfit. He wants some saddle soap for his boots."

"Can do."

"Fertig just wants soap, any kind so long as it doesn't turn his hair red."

Guerrillas are very clean in their personal habits. The lack of soap, a real item, bothered them greatly at first. Casting about to meet this crisis, they had found that lye could be produced by burning coconut palms, lime from roasting coral or sea shells. Blending these two ingredients with coconut oil resulted in a fine, free-lathering soap—good for its purpose but hard on clothes and tending to dye the hair a brilliant henna.

"Soap for Fertig," Colonel Whitney wrote. "Next."

"Here's one for Dental Supply," said Chick, his eyes twinkling.

The colonel laid down his pencil.

"Now don't tell me the boys want toothbrushes and toothpaste?"

"No, they're doing all right with coconut fiber and sea salt," said Chick, who had found this guerrilla method of cleansing the teeth eminently satisfactory. "While Colonel Kangleon was in prison he lost about forty pounds. His gums shrank. Consequently his store teeth don't fit him anymore. We've either got to get him a new set or some stickum."

"It'll have to be stickum. There's no way of making jaw impressions by short wave, is there?"

"None that I know of."

The colonel promised to see what he could do about the Leyte chieftain's teeth. Then he surveyed Chick in silence for a while, his face sober.

"Chick," he began, "here at headquarters we don't like the idea of your running around the jungle, in and out of Jap lines, without a weapon."

"I'm no commando," Chick objected.

"I know you're not, but you ought to carry side arms anyway. Supposing you get in a spot?"

"Colonel, I spend most of my time and energy trying to avoid spots."

"But you just might run into trouble unexpectedly."

"Yes, I might." Chick considered this thoughtfully. "I will carry a gun ... on one condition."

"Name it."

"Get me a weapon equipped with a rear-view mirror," Chick said, adding with a grin, "so I can fire while running."

Some weeks later Commander Parsons found a requisition on his desk, returned from Ordnance, for "One Thompson Submachine Gun, Caliber .45, equipped with rear-view mirror." At the bottom a serious clerk had typed:

"No evidence can be found in Ordnance catalogues to cover item."

"The guerrilla plan of operation, together with a plan for guerrilla supply, was worked out between Colonel Whitney and Commander Parsons on his return from the Islands, and presented to General MacArthur, who wholeheartedly approved it. It had two main objectives: to set up coast-watcher stations for the Navy, together with Intelligence units for the Army; and to supply the guerrillas with everything they needed for their type of warfare against the Japanese. This would be tangible and material proof to "Juan de la Cruz"—the Filipino man in the street—that the Aid was really on its way.

Until this time there had been no effort on the part of Southwest Pacific Headquarters to counteract Japanese propaganda in any way. Colonel Whitney, after studying the situation in the Islands, and using information brought down by Parsons, decided to recommend to General MacArthur a simple form of propaganda based upon the idea of plugging a single phrase by way of answer to enemy propaganda.

This brief phrase was: "I shall return." Even briefer was the general's reaction.

"Okay," he penciled at the bottom of the request.

Henceforth every pack of cigarettes, gum or chocolate candy, every pencil, sewing kit, and other small homey article which Commander Parsons was to take into the Islands would bear this single line, without comment or elaboration.

"I shall return," signed "MacArthur."

Volumes could not have said more to the Filipinos.

From the beginning of the organization of Spyron Chick had realized that to fill a requisition for guerrilla supplies in Australia would be one thing: to deliver those supplies safely into the hands of the jungle fighters, quite another. Here the Navy stepped into the picture in a role fully as important as that of the Army, and far more hazardous. Andin Captain A. H. McCollum Chick enlisted another friend whose sympathy for and co-operation in assisting the Filipino cause was to prove fully as great as that of Colonel Whitney.

"To these two great men," in Chick's words, "Spyron owes everything."

As soon as Spyron was set up and ready to begin moving its supplies Captain McCollum was able to obtain the support of Admiral Christie in making available space on outward-bound submarines. When the first few trips resulted in the transfer of only a pittance of materiel, it was Captain McCollum to whom Chick confided his dream and burning ambition—to persuade the Navy to assign Spyron a large cargo-carrying under seas craft with the sole function of supplying the guerrillas.

"You realize what you are asking, Commander?" the captain said gravely when Chick brought this proposition to his desk.

Chick, equally grave, nodded.

"How about asking the Navy to give Spyron the exclusive use of a most important unit of war, to equip a group of men who haven't yet proved themselves in the eyes of the world—but who will?"

"You're sure of that?"

"Absolutely. Get the stuff to the guerrillas in sufficient quantities and they'll pay off one hundred per cent. Look at the information regarding the movement of enemy shipping that is already pouring into H.Q. from the handful of coast-watcher stations now operating and the figures of Jap shipping sunk as direct result of this information. Picture a hundred coast-watcher stations instead of a dozen, a hundred thousand guerrillas armed with rifles instead of a few thousands . . .

Captain McCollum interrupted, with a smile. "I was only asking," he said, and looked at Chick's earnest face curiously. "Where'd you get this boundless confidence in the little brown men?"

"When you live with a guy twenty years you learn to know him pretty well," said Chick quietly. "The Filipino has what it takes. He's got guts—but he needs more than that."

"We'll see that he gets it," said the captain.

Within a matter of weeks Commander Parsons stood on the deck of one of the largest United States cargo-carrying submarines—built many years before, but still full of life, and more recently turned over to Spyron through Chick's persuasiveness and determination and the energetic sponsorship of Captain McCollum. Below decks were more supplies than could have been carried by a dozen operational subs. The commanding officer of this first submarine assigned to Spyron activities was Commander Frank Latta, whose bravery and keenness for his work were to be demonstrated time and time again on subsequent missions.

The Aid is really coming now, thought Chick happily, and in a big way. Then he grew sober as he remembered his own terrific responsibility in this latest venture.

"We are taking at face value your recommendations regarding the operation of this submarine," the captain had stated. "We are depending on you almost entirely for details concerning destination, affairs at destination, the safeguarding of the vessel, and its sure dispatch without harm from guerrilla areas. In navigating a submarine," he concluded, "you never make two mistakes. Just one is too many."

Commander Parsons may from time to time have appeared careless of his own life. Never of the lives of others. With utmost care, in a secret exchange of messages with guerrilla-held territories, he now worked out his destinations, weighing every possible factor for success and safety.

Ease of approach to and departure from a rendezvous site were of paramount importance. Likewise complete hourly knowledge of enemy movements on land, sea, and sky. Schedules must be extremely flexible to permit new contact points with the guerrillas should the enemy turn up unexpectedly.

In this, as in all pioneering endeavors of Spyron, Chick would go along himself.

"There is nothing more vulnerable than a submarine on the surface or in shallow water," Captain McCollum reminded him as Chick went aboard the cargo carrier for its first trip in November 1943.

"I know something about that, Captain," said Chick.

What he didn't know Commander Parsons was to learn immediately— and the hard way.

CHAPTER IX

FOR SOME REASON, ON THIS FIRST TRIP OF THE CARGO CARRIER, we had a lot of closer shaves than usual. The last one was due more to my own stupidity than anything else.

Chick's itinerary was both extensive and ambitious. He wished to look in on Samar, Negros, and Cebu to verify, at firsthand, rumors of strong guerrilla movements on these important islands, and to do whatever was necessary to bring these forces under individual leaders. Supplies must be dropped at Panay, Leyte, and Mindanao, whose leaders had already been recognized by General MacArthur. Coast-watcher radio stations must be set up at strategic points, especially on the island of Mindoro.

Typically, Chick decided to tackle the latter and hardest assignment first. Mindoro lies right across Verde Island Passage from Luzon, hardly twenty-five miles from Batangas Peninsula. The proposed site for the coast-watcher station on that island was literally under the very noses of the Japanese. Directly toward this danger spot the submarine now proceeded.

In addition to radio equipment and officer personnel to man the various proposed stations, the sub carried the first group of graduates from Tabragalba—the school outside of Brisbane stocked by Colonel Whitney and headed by Lieutenant Colonel Louis Brown, stepson of General Harboard.

Once clear of the headlands of Australia, Chick looked over the eager brown faces of these American-born Filipinos. None of them had ever been aboard a submarine before. Some of them had never even visited the Philippine Islands. Most of them were over thirty and all completely aware of what would happen to them if they should fall into the hands of the Japanese while serving as guerrilla coast watchers.

Yet eagerly and willingly these American and Hawaiian-born Filipinos had volunteered for this most hazardous of duties. By comparison the ordinary guerrilla fighter seemed footloose and fancy free.

Fortunately, Chick mused, most of them don't know what they're in for. And he thought of the endless days these men would have to stay on the job, in exposed positions, without adequate guerrilla coverage.

These boys—and Chick Parsons—were now to have a premature and unexpected test of courage. A test which very nearly nipped the new venture—and its leader—in the bud.

The cargo sub, as was customary, carried loaded torpedo tubes, ammunition for its deck guns. It was ready and willing to tackle the enemy wherever he should be encountered. And on this particular voyage, on the night of November tenth, there came to the skipper a message from the sub base on the Baker schedule to the effect that a large enemy tanker could be expected in the area we were known to be approaching. The sub was told to alter course if necessary in order to intercept the tanker and attack it. According to calculations given by the sub base, the tanker should approach our position in the Mindanao Sea about 10 P. M. the following night. In order to make the interception the sub had to slow down and get set for what everyone on board hoped would be a fat kill. The sub cruised submerged to charge batteries and start preparing for an interesting night. All hands were nervously vigilant for any sign of an enemy craft.

About eleven-thirty came the message: "Captain, it's coming right along, and might be the target we've been waiting for."

To the bridge, the captain advised: "Keep a keen lookout and report when target sighted."

The captain and Chick went to the bridge, each with binoculars, and then began a keen lookout for the first sight of what turned out soon to be the shadow of a very large vessel.

"Give that a gander, Chick," said Frank. "Isn't that pretty sight?"

Chick shortly afterward picked up the target in his glasses—apparently a Jap tanker, seemingly without escort, wallowing through the Mindanao Sea, low in the water from her full load of oil.

"Very beautiful. When are you going to make an approach? "

"Right now," and with that Captain Latta ordered the bridge cleared, gave the diving alarm, and took the ship to periscope depth, with instructions to all to prepare for an attack.

"All tubes forward, get ready for firing."

As the signal lights in the conning tower showed the tubes ready for firing, the skipper tracked the target in the periscope, listening to the data being called off by the officer next to him. Parsons was an interested watcher of this procedure, though he had nothing to do with the maneuver. He would have, however, had there been a chance to surface and fight, as he was assigned to the 20-mm. guns on the bridge.

Captain Latta, as is customary aboard the subs, gave a running talk to the men aboard through the loud-speaker system, telling them:

"Men, here we have a chance to sink another of the Emperor's babies. She looks like a million dollars two weeks after pay day. She couldn't come on a better course if we'd set it for her. If nothing happens we can let go with a few on her next 'zig.' It won't be long now. Keep your fingers crossed, for here goes. . . ."

Latta called for the tubes to be fired in order. The buttons were pressed and he heard the report: "One away . . ."

"Two away . . ."

"That should do the trick. If only one hits her we won't have to bother much more with her."

The long white fingers of the four torpedoes reached through Mindanao Sea, clutched the Jap tanker and crushed it into roaring flame. The captain gave a grunt of satisfaction and was about to give the order to surface when a muffled crackling and rending beat against the sides of the submarine and the lights winked a warning.

The faces of Chick and the captain grew taut. Too well they knew that sound. His knuckles suddenly white, the skipper gripped the periscope handles, sweeping the horizon.

"Enemy surface craft approaching at 190 true."

"Rig for diving," shouted the captain into the interphone. To Chick he added: "Jap destroyers. Apparently hidden behind that island while we were attacking the tanker."

Frantically the submarine sought sanctuary. The sub sought to shake the depth bombs that rained down about it.

In the galley crockery crashed. A small hail of paint flakes showered down. The lights danced and flickered. The jarring grew heavier.

The anxious face of Captain Latta swept before Chick's eyes.

"The ash cans seem to be getting closer," he said. "What do you think, Frank?"

The young skipper listened a moment to the jarring. "There's only one thing to do, Chick. Surface and run for it, hoping we can shake them in the dark."

He brought the vessel to the surface. The Diesels took hold with a steady throb.

"Full speed ahead," the captain ordered the engine room, and the beat accelerated.

Darkness was coming on. They had a fair start. But submarines do not outrun destroyers.

"Send one of your Filipino boys to the bridge as stern watcher, Chick," the skipper ordered.

A little brown man eagerly scrambled up the tower. Shortly he reported: "There are friends behind, blinking at us."

Chick scrambled up and had a look. As he did so miniature geysers of water shot up not far to port and starboard.

"That's a hell of a way to advertise friendship," he said. "Those are Jap guns, son."

The Filipino boy dropped his head.

"Sorry, sir."

"That's okay," said Chick, slapping him on the shoulder.

In the engine room, Lieutenant Plummet, the engineer officer, looked with growing apprehension at his gauges. Called the bridge.

"Is it necessary to keep the engines going at this pace?" he inquired.

"How fast are you going?"

"A knot and a half faster than possible," came the reply. The captain smiled grimly.

"Keep it there or you won't need engines," he said. "They're coming at us like the hammers of hell."

An hour passed, while the Diesels raced themselves into white heat, and the shells fell ever closer to the submarine. Up ahead, off in the distance, strange low-lying lights danced, close to the water, seeming to come from the very sea.

"What do you make of that, Chick?" the skipper asked.

Chick glanced at the map. "Fishermen. Now if we just circle around here . . ." Chick drew a finger along the map.

The captain had traveled with Chick before. Without a word he changed course.

"Everybody," Chick recalls, "drew a long breath and we went on our way."

It was with considerable relief to all concerned that the submarine finally made destination—a bay in an isolated section which appeared to have no strategic interest to the enemy. Appearances, however, proved deceiving.

Arriving offshore about midnight, Chick Parsons went into his customary routine. A rubber boat was launched and with a young Filipino soldier to help paddle Chick started ashore.

On the way in he made out a graceful Filipino sailboat known as a batel, riding tranquilly at anchor. Having a carrying capacity of about forty tons, it was ideally suited for the transporting of supplies by the guerrillas. And if for the guerrillas, why not for the coast-watcher equipment and personnel we have aboard, thought Chick?

Paddling over, Commander Parsons quickly climbed to the deck by means of a ladder hanging overboard. Everybody appeared to be asleep except a sentry, leaning against the rail. This guard immediately challenged Chick—in Japanese.

"I was too surprised to run," Chick remembers, "and merely stood staring at him while figures on deck about my feet began to stir. Then the sentry made a move and I dashed for the rail. As I was approaching the side someone rose from the dark. Whether he had a knife or bayonet in his hand I do not know to this day. Anyway I got it in the chin as I started over the side.

"I told the Filipino paddler to get the hell out of there in a hurry, which he needed no second invitation to do. Theme on board fired at the lad in the rubber boat but failed to hit him. I escaped undetected by swimming as fast as possible and staying underwater as long as I could. In this manner we both got safely ashore, where I found that the area was Jap-patrolled and the sailboat there, apparently, for the purpose of buying supplies from the natives."

Guerrillas were also in the area and as usual had a very complete military outfit, including medics. Some of the best-known physicians and trained nurses in the Islands had gone to the hills and offered their services to the leaders of the free movement. Working without adequate medicines or equipment, prior to Spyron shipments, these people had even established hospitals and clinics not only for the guerrillas but for the civilians of the surrounding areas. They also accompanied the guerrillas in their movements against the enemy, and Mindoro, Chick now learned to his advantage, was no exception to the rule.

"My chin," Commander Parsons concludes, "was pretty bad. There was a deep cut, bleeding badly, but ashore I was able to get first aid from a young guerrilla medic, who pulled the wound together with an expertly placed bandage, which held very well until I got back aboard the sub. On the sub the corpsman took pride in sticking the wound together in such a way that it would show little or no scar—a bit of plastic surgery, he called it. In the morning, to my pleasure and amazement, the batel weighed anchor and we were able to accomplish our mission despite the fact that I had boarded a Jap vessel and even attempted to enlist the aid of the Japanese in getting our supplies ashore—a very difficult diplomatic maneuver in wartime."

Dropping off coast-watcher personnel and equipment at one spot after another, chosen by Chick Parsons, the big cargo sub nosed down through the myriad islands of the archipelago. In taking leave of each brave little group of Filipinos and Americans, Chick felt a twinge of regret. Some, he knew, would lose their lives—like Merc Phillips, who died in his attempt to establish a Mindoro station and contact Manila, and Sergeant Corpus, who stuck to his isolated post until the Japanese ended his services to the guerrilla cause.

Others would find the strain and isolation too much for their nerves and reason would totter. Many would have to carry on, month after month, in the most barren and isolated of regions, without help or relief. Truman Hemingway of Panaon and Dinagat islands. Johnny Johnson, who stayed in the Davao Gulf from 1943 through the invasion. And dozens of others.

Chick felt like a judge passing indeterminate sentence on these brave Filipinos and Americans, but it had to be done. In his own words: "There was only one way to find out what the Japs were up to—and our coast-watcher network was the answer. It was the very heartbeat of the guerrilla movement and in the long run paid off beautifully—thanks to the loyalty and self-sacrifice of these men who were true patriots, true guerrillas, and true heroes in every sense of the word."

CHAPTER X

I FOUND THAT SOME OF THE ISLANDS WERE SWINGING BEAUTIFULLY into line under strong individual leaders. Others, because of jealousy and strife between the aspirants, could not be recognized as unified districts until just before invasion.

It had not been possible, of course, for Commander Parsons to visit all the major islands of the Philippines on his original expedition. Working his way south from Mindoro with the cargo carrier, however, Chick was able to secure a much broader overall picture of guerrilla activities and organizations as he contacted, in order, Panay, Samar, Negros, and Cebu.

Macario Peralta—the leader on Panay who first acquainted the outside world with the existence of a free movement in the Islands—Chick found to have a much larger force of men than anticipated, about twelve thousand. These men had been solidly welded together into a fine fighting unit by Peralta and with the assistance of one of the outstanding national figures in Philippine affairs, Tomas Confesor.

Former governor of Iloilo and prominent in the Islands for years, Confesor refused to surrender to the Japanese. Taking to the hills, he continued to develop a free movement and resist the enemy to the utmost. Despite offers of a very tempting nature from the Japanese, this patriot remained steadfast to his ideals and gave immeasurable help to Colonel Peralta.

Peralta had already indicated his willingness to recognize General MacArthur, and Commander Parsons found nothing to do on Panay but drop supplies and push on to Samar.

Here Chick encountered a quite different situation.

Samar is large. Large enough, Chick was appraised, for four leaders with strong personal support to contest for supremacy of the guerrilla movement on that island. Most of the trouble, it seemed, stemmed from the north, where a former member of the Philippine constabulary scrapped continually with the other leader, a former governor.

"This former constabulary officer," Chick's informants reported, "is a bad actor. He has terrorized the people and has commandeered much equipment not needed by him or his forces."

"Commander"—a foreshortened form of the word "commandeer"—was another English word adopted by the people of the Philippines. It meant "to take by force or without payment." In the early days many guerrilla leaders had recourse to this method of acquiring materiel. It was a universal practice of the Japanese, who would either pay for the seized property with Jap invasion currency or else give a vague promise to replace at some future date, evidenced only by a receipt signed by a Japanese officer.

General MacArthur, informed by Commander Parsons that some of the guerrilla leaders had recourse to this process which alienated them from the body of the people, was strongly against such procedure. He wished the guerrillas to pay for what they needed and to that end Chick had brought in funds against which recognized guerrilla chieftains could draw up their own money.

First, however, it was necessary to be able to recognize a single leader and a unified area. Samar had neither.

The leader in Samar, furthermore, proved unwilling to have radio coast-watcher stations set up on his premises. He threatened to ambush and kill any men sent up for that purpose.

Charlie Smith was selected by General MacArthur to go into Samar and set up an important radio control net and a center from which could be sent a number of intelligence-seeking units to various parts of Luzon and Samar. In issuing the call letters for his control radio station, the Signal Section significantly gave the letters M.A.C.A., which are the letters used by General MacArthur in initialing staff papers. Charlie was particularly suited for this mission by reason of his bravery and his refusal to be moved by threats from any of the local guerrilla leaders. He landed with the party, made his way immediately into the hinterland, and managed to disperse his various stations and men before his first encounter with the enemy, which was almost disastrous. Charlie held out in Samar and kept on the air with his M.A.C.A. station from January 1944 through the date of the invasion.

About a month before the invasion it was decided to appoint Charlie as the district commander of Samar, with the hope and prayer that he would be able to unify the different elements on the island and weld them into a fighting force which would assist the Americans on D-Day.

Charlie was able to do quite a bit in that connection, and on D-Day was ready to put men in the field to harass the enemy.

There were at least four separate major guerrilla groups on the Islands. Two in the north led by former Governor Arteche, who was subsequently killed by the Japanese, and Captain Merritt, formerly of the Philippine constabulary. From the south were Captains Abia and Valley. The two lads in the south were mutually friendly and willing to recognize a higher authority. Neither was strong enough in men, arms, or leadership to be given the area command.

On Negros, Major Jess Villamor, Philippine born, had made considerable progress toward unifying the three chief guerrilla groups. Villamor left Lieutenant Colonel Abcede to continue this process and bring it to ultimate success.

That, Commander Parsons thought as Negros dropped into the sea behind the sub, leaves only Cebu of the larger islands to be recognized. Chick knew pretty well what he would find on this strategic island, where the guerrilla movement was unlike that anywhere else.

Captains in USAFFE at Cebu were James P. Cushing, a former mining engineer, and his friend Harry Fenton, prior to the war well known as a conductor of radio programs and manager of the Cebu radio station. At the surrender these two men started the guerrilla movement on this island as co-commanders: Fenton the administrative head, Cushing the fighting commander.

Gushing was considerably worried by the actions of his partner. He was death on puppets, literally and figuratively.

At the time of the occupation of the Islands by the Japanese the average citizen—not an out-and-out guerrilla—fell into one of three fairly definite classes of sympathy and action.

A number were puppets in every sense of the word. Definitely pro-Japanese, they came out openly against the Americans and in praise of the invaders. In gratitude the Japanese elevated these men to positions of public trust.

Laurel, whom the Japs had set up as president, was shot and wounded while playing golf on the Wackwack course, just outside Manila. Andong Roces, son of a prominent Manila publisher whose paper was completely Jap-controlled, was killed with his wife while coming out of a Manila movie theater. Likewise General Ricarte, partner of General Aguinaldo in the Spanish-American War and subsequent insurrection. Ricarte, renouncing his country and fleeing to Tokyo, had been returned to Manila at the time of Pearl Harbor and set up as a puppet official. He was shot while making a speech in an outlying town, and while practically on his deathbed for a couple of months, he eventually recovered.

There were others. There would be more.

The vast army of civil service employees and minor officials, both in city and provincial governments, were also part of the puppet set up. However, they could not be considered pro-Japanese or true collaborators just because they considered it necessary to continue making a living in the only occupations they knew.

The third class of civilians consisted of leading politicians and officials who had been left behind by the retiring administration with instructions to carry on the interests of the Filipino people as best they could. These men continued to lead a comfortable existence in their own homes, had plenty of food, the use of their automobiles, and drew salaries from the puppet administration. But they gave no more assistance to the enemy than their position called for.

A lot of them were secretly aiding the guerrilla movement by securing information about the Japs in their towns and transmitting it to acknowledged guerrilla heads in the hills.

They were in a position to do the cause much good but Fenton couldn't see it. He felt that anyone who worked for or with the Japanese in any capacity whatever was a puppet, and his course of action was summary execution.

Pushing on across Mindanao Sea, Chick confided his worry about the situation on Cebu to Colonel Fertig, who presently put him in touch with a clerk who had kept the records of Fenton's executions.

There were more than a hundred names on the list, many of them persons whose characters were above reproach. All of the victims had friends. The handwriting on the wall became quite clear to Commander Parsons. He bided his time and waited for the inevitable. It came, more quickly than he had anticipated, with word from Cushing that Fenton had been assassinated by his own chief of staff.

Shortly after the assassination of Fenton and a couple of mopping-up expeditions on the part of the Japanese which kept Gushing pretty much inactive, Colonel Whitney, backed by the recommendations of Colonel Fertig and Parsons, recommended to General MacArthur that Cushing be named the Cebu area commander, which was done. General MacArthur gave the recognition, Cebu fell in line, and another island front was cleared of internal strife and ready to devote wholehearted attention to the real enemy.

In guerrilla areas today feelings are tense, pressure is great at times, and life does not have the high value of peacetimes. Tolerance for Fenton and his methods ran out, as it has also run out for many of the real puppets and will for more before this is over. It does not seem possible that we shall escape a macanza, a blood bath, in the Philippine Islands.

CHAPTER XI

SYSTEMATICALLY THE JAPANESE ENDEAVORED TO WRECK the economic life of the Philippine Islands. With equal persistence the guerrillas tried to maintain and build it up.

To export everything out of a country and import nothing, to close schools, business houses, food and clothing stores, shut off public utilities, halt transportation, bar theaters, ban radios, and then speak glowingly of the benefits of collaboration with the authors of these privations is a process which only a Jap or Nazi could expect to appeal to a liberty-loving people.

Toward the end of 1943 and the beginning of '44 large numbers of the Kempeitai, the Jap secret police, were removed from the streets of occupied towns. Various public officials had been continued in office, and under President Laurel the people were given a semblance of independent government. Yet these were only empty gestures. There is no reason to believe that the Filipinos, barring puppets and opportunists, could possibly have been seduced into a collaborative frame of mind in the face of what actually happened to them under Jap rule.

In order to acquaint himself with the picture in occupied as well as unoccupied areas of the Philippines, Commander Parsons summoned to him, just before his return to Australia at the close of 1943, one of the most prominent members of his Luzon Intelligence net. Just how Chick established a spy network in Manila and on heavily held Luzon is a story which cannot now be related. That he wound into this ring some of the most influential Filipinos is an established fact.

By devious means a prominent statesman who had served his country well in many peacetime activities—now as spy—made his way to Colonel Fertig's Mindanao headquarters and was presently closeted with Chick Parsons.

"And how," Chick opened the interview, "is Co-Prosperity on Luzon?"

"It does not exist, Commander," came the answer. "The puppets are in clover. The people walk in fear and poverty. The Japanese make no effort to keep them decently clothed, housed, transported, or healthy. Merely to exist, one must belong to the Kalibapi, the Japanese Neighborhood Association. Belonging, one automatically becomes a spy for the Rising Sun."

Chick knew something about this wily arrangement the invaders had devised to keep civilians in the occupied sections firmly under their thumb. Every town was divided into districts, districts into sections, sections into the smallest unit—ten families or ten houses. The leader of each group was responsible for the actions of every member in his group. He must report the exact number of individuals under his ten roofs. If the Kempeitai discovered an extra person in a group—an agent, visitor, or person with no logical reason for his presence—it went very badly with the leader, sometimes with his whole family.

"Fort Santiago has swallowed up many men loyal to the cause. Few return from the dungeons there."

"I know," Chick said quietly. "The Kalibapi makes it difficult to circulate agents in occupied towns."

"Si," his old friend nodded. "It is difficult to persuade those, who otherwise would be helpful, that they have a higher duty to their country than to their families. I am afraid we may count on very little help from the man in the street—when those streets are under the rule of the Neighborhood Association and the Kempeitai."

Chick was to find a way around this obstacle before he was through. He continued his questions.

"How is the food situation in cities like Manila?"

"It is very bad. Commander. The black market, sponsored by our friends the Chinese, who control the retail stores, flourishes. Rice is up to one thousand pesos a bag and going higher. The Chinese hesitate at nothing to discredit their enemies in the eyes of the Filipino people."

"Good. And what are the Japanese economists doing about this?"

"They have had to take over the food situation in the larger towns and more populated districts, bringing in food from outside. This has necessitated a system of distribution amounting practically to a dole, in order to bring food within reach of the average laborer."

"I understand that the peon, the laborer who received one peso per day and no food before the war, now receives five pesos and food for his daily services."

"True, but what good is the extra money? A man may buy a woman for a night, he may gamble, hoping to treble his stake and so purchase something on the black market. Otherwise there is nothing to buy. Inflation is advancing rapidly."

By the end of 1943 practically none of the old Philippine money remained in circulation. It had all been withdrawn and hoarded. But there was in circulation some two hundred million pesos—one hundred million dollars' worth—of Japanese invasion scrip with Jap presses whirring day and night turning out more.

To speed the process of inflation and knock the wobbly props out from under the Jap economic structure in the Philippines, Chick had brought with him huge amounts of counterfeit invasion scrip which his agents cleverly slipped into the currency stream. General MacArthur wished to force the Japanese either to revise their entire currency situation or to set up bread lines for payment in food instead of cash. "MacArthur even planned to load bombers with spurious invasion scrip and dump the money wholesale over occupied areas if inflation did not proceed swiftly enough.

This, however, was not necessary. Inflation in the Philippines took care of itself, due to the collapse of the law of supply and demand. There was too much money, too little to buy.

"Here in guerrilla territories," Chick explained with satisfaction, "there is no inflation." Japanese invasion scrip was used only in the occupied areas. Aware of the need for a respected currency in the unoccupied regions, President Quezon gave the provincial governments permission and authority to print money for administration operations. These provincial governments continued to function from the hills as soon as General MacArthur could recognize a true guerrilla organization.

Along with immense sums of counterfeit money, there was brought in real cash not only to finance governmental operations but against which guerrilla chieftains could make requisition in order to print their own money. This enabled them to buy, rather than seize, what they needed—and to pay their way into the hearts and confidence of the people of the Islands.

Writing paper, old governmental forms, Manila wrapping paper, and even toilet tissue was the basis of guerrilla currency. Berry juice was often times used in place of ink and the money was crudely printed. However, currency issued by one guerrilla area was acceptable in another and par was religiously maintained in confident expectation of full redemption on release of the Islands.

"Not only is there no inflation in the unoccupied sections," Chick continued, "but also there is no black market or profiteering. Ceiling prices are rigorously maintained and anyone endeavoring to profit by the situation is dealt with summarily by the guerrilla chiefs."

"The people of the unoccupied areas are lucky." His visitor nodded. "Here at least they can till the soil and raise their sustenance. They do not have to turn traitor in order to feed their little ones."

"The guerrilla leaders are not only feeding their own men but in many instances the people of the countryside."

Colonel Fertig, for instance, had realized how important to his movement was the friendship of the people, how necessary not to strain their hospitality too far. His beachguards were continually picking up doubtful characters without adequate passes or explanation of their business in his territory. These men were interned and sent inland to farms. Here they tended herds of cattle and raised vegetables such as yams, beans, corn.

"Corn?" The senator raised his eyebrows. "That is for the hill people, the very poor."

"It was," Chick corrected him, "before the Japanese took over the rice paddies along the coast. Corn can be ground down into grits and grits will sustain life. The banana, sliced thin, baked to a hard mass over charcoal and pulverized, becomes flour. Tuba and potatoes yield yeast."

His visitor sighed. "Ah, for the good days when for our hemp, our hardwoods and fiber plants we received in return the real articles of import—canned meats, flour, yeast, coffee."

"Those days will come again, Senator," Chick assured him. "And soon."

"If you say it, Commander, it must be so. You have given us hope, and hope is sometimes more necessary to life than food." He started to rise. Chick restrained him, his face thoughtful.

"One more question, amigo. Do you"—he hesitated—"have any news of a certain lady? Mrs. Jurika, the mother of Tommy and Katsy?"

The senator dropped his eyes.

"I was afraid you would ask me that and had you not I must tell you anyhow," he said slowly. "When our plan for the escape from the Islands of a certain person of importance was revealed to the Japanese by a traitor, many were arrested, Mrs. Jurika was among them. She was sentenced to thirty-five years in prison."

Chick took a couple of quick steps up and down the porch in his agitation. "But she has no connection with any spy ring," he objected.

"For supuesto, no. But she has a very definite connection"—the senator raised his dark eyes—"with one Commander Parsons who is valued highly by the Japanese."

Chick thought of his promise to Tommy Jurika, even now laboring for Spyron in Australia.

"If I could only have persuaded her to come out with us when she had the chance," he groaned.

"Her home is here. She is a mother and her son, she thought, was in the hands of the Japanese. Surely you can understand. . . ."

"Yes, of course. I know, too, that it would be fatal for her if I should try to help directly. But you must do everything possible for her."

His visitor looked surprised that Chick should ask such a question. "Madre Jurika is in no immediate danger," he said.

"Her guards are loyal Filipinos. They know what to do. . . if the Japanese show signs of molesting her."

Chick looked relieved.

"Gracias, amigo" he said. "Perhaps later I can do something."

"Later will be time for all things," said the senator as he rose to his feet. "We may not meet again, Chico, on the soil of our beloved Islands," he said prophetically, "but it is of nothing. The individual is of no importance. Only the cause. Nothing can stop it now."

The senator was right on both counts. The Japanese, learning of his membership in the spy ring, severed this connection with one stroke of a Samurai sword.

But they could not break the chain. They only drew it tighter about their own throats.

The true story of the contribution of these patriots on Luzon may never be told. Suffice it to say it was very great. Without the sacrifice of these men, General MacArthur's campaign would have been far more difficult and costly in the lives of American servicemen.

The pay scale of the guerrilla soldier approximates that of the American fighting man. To avoid the possibility of inflation and profiteering in guerrilla areas, the leaders gave their men only a partial pay, ranging from ten pesos per month for privates to one hundred and fifty per month for field officers.

Humorously the guerrillas called their currency "ting-hoy"—meaning "counterfeit" or "useless"—since there was so little to buy. Some extra food, laundry, perhaps a bit of candy made by the Women's Auxiliary Service which functioned in every guerrilla camp and town, failed to exhaust the funds of the guerrilla soldiers. Presently one of the leaders came to Chick and said:

"Commander, my boys have accumulated quite a little pay. They wish to put this money into United States war bonds to help the effort."

Chick gathered requests for bonds wherever he went and on his return to Australia carried thousands of pesos' worth of applications. Unfortunately the difficulty, not only of registering bonds but of determining what credit was available to the people of the Islands, made it impossible to accept these applications from guerrillas and patriotic civilians. Nevertheless the desire of the Filipinos to offer their small sums as well as their blood to the cause of democracy was most touching.

And nowhere was this loyalty more powerfully expressed than in the attitude of the Filipinos toward Commander Parsons himself—not only as a personal friend, but as a naval officer and representative of a beloved nation. Of this loyalty Chick says: "While the price on my head rose to a hundred thousand pesos—fifty thousand dollars and a staggering sum to the average Filipino—I was never betrayed to the enemy. I was constantly sheltered and protected by strangers for no other reason than that I was an American, and in their full knowledge that they would be executed if caught in this act by the Japanese."

CHAPTER XII

LACKING AN IMPORT-EXPORT TRADE, GUERRILLA CHIEFS like Colonel Fertig built up a land and sea trade between various areas for the exchange of goods. Often on mountain trails I stepped aside to let a caravan of a hundred or more laden carabaos pass. At night the dark passages between the Islands were ghostly with sails as the fleet plied its growing commerce.

The guerrillas had a terrific responsibility in the receipt of the cargo delivered to them by the cargo-carrying submarines. It was essential that this cargo be received rapidly and dispersed to all parts of the area as rapidly as possible. To do this, the guerrillas built up for resupply to the various units, and for dispersal of the cargo, a guerrilla fleet of sailboats which eventually assumed substantial proportions.

Always one step ahead of the Japanese, the guerrillas developed this maritime trade in relative immunity at first by utilizing a simple formula. "No matter what happens," was their nautical code, "go on about your business."

On one memorable occasion in December 1943 Commander Parsons found this philosophy hard to apply.

Chick had started this voyage with some Filipinos at night, expecting to reach destination and deliver his good sunder safe cover of darkness. However, during the night the wind fell. Frantic paddling found the party still some eight or nine miles from shore when the sun rose.

At this point a Japanese patrol launch, returning to base, rounded a headland on a course calculated to take it well within a hundred yards of the sailing canoe.

Commander Parsons' hair is dark brown. His skin, at this time, was well tanned and he was dressed like a Filipino. But close scrutiny could not fail to reveal his round face and sturdy physique as that of an outsider.

Involuntarily he started to turn the rudder.

"No, no, Commander," breathed the young skipper whom he was spelling. "For Dios, do not alter the course visibly. A fraction only."

Yielding to greater experience and wisdom in this type of encounter, Chick veered the tiller very slightly, so as to clear the launch as widely as possible without giving the impression of trying to avoid it.

On came the patrol boat, revealing six or seven soldiers snoozing in the shade of the machine guns on deck.

The young skipper patted Chick's leg in encouragement. The crew of the little dalama, or sailboat, made an elaborate pretense of mending the heavy net which hid the radio equipment they were carrying. The heat of the day did not justify the sweat that began to pour down Chick's body as the patrol boat came nearer.

"We passed," he concludes this story, "at one hundred yards, which seemed to me like six inches. In fact, at one point, I thought the launch was going to run us down. The Japs gave us a careful once-over, apparently saw nothing unusual about us, and went on their way.

"We had two guns lying in the cockpit and passed close enough to fire, but we could not have hoped to compete with the machine guns mounted on the deck of the enemy. Besides which, as usual, I had not the slightest desire to tangle with the Japs."

As the guerrilla fleet multiplied and increased, the Japanese began to catch on. They became keenly interested in sea traffic and presently, whenever they saw a laden vessel—regardless of who was in it—they would turn in pursuit. If any attempt was made to get away the Japs would fire until all hands were either killed or wounded. If there was no resistance they would approach and grab onto the boat with a long boathook or a piece of bamboo with a crook in the end of it.

"We got hooked by the Japs," a young skipper explained to Chick, somewhat later, on being asked why he had not shown up on time—and this phrase also took its place in the new wartime language of the guerrillas.

"What did they do to you?" Chick wanted to know.

"Oh, the usual." The youngster grinned. "Towed us into base and asked many foolish questions about our strength and positions."

"You answered?"

"For Dios, yes. Otherwise, it means the torture. But what did I tell them?" He laughed. "That is another story."

To counteract the "hooking" and sinking of individual vessels and assure greater security Colonel Fertig developed a convoy system for his fleet, sending his vessels out in groups of ten. As heavier arms were supplied Fertig mounted 20-, 30-, and 50-millimeter machine guns on his launches and dalamas—and finally 20- and 30-millimeter cannon.

One of his skippers had already demonstrated to Commander Parsons what he could do, and with homemade armament at that. This captain, whose name was Zapanta, was the skipper of the main guerrilla resupply vessel, the Athena. In the early days of the historic voyages of the Athena she had only a homemade 3-inch cannon and a couple of worn-out .30-caliber water-cooled machine guns. This situation was cleared up quickly, however, by supplying the Athena with a 20-millimeter submarine type deck gun which proudly replaced the 3-inch monstrosity. With this additional firepower, and with Zapanta in command, the Athena became quite cocky—on one occasion actually engaging two Jap patrol launches and a destroyer escort off Surigao Point. Zapanta scored hits on all three, sank one of the launches, and the other two fled.

Another quite famous guerrilla escort craft was facetiously named the So What. This vessel was skippered by a youngster who was formerly a junior officer in the Philippine Merchant Marine. His unit was also armed with 20-millimeter cannon and .50-caliber machine guns. While not looking for encounters with the enemy, So What was sufficiently confident of its ability not to run from an engagement. The So What was attacked by a patrol launch or destroyer escort near Butuan Bay and put up a good scrap, but not without considerable damage to the guerrilla craft. The So What, however, was successful in engaging the enemy craft until the supply sailboat she was escorting could arrive safely at a near-by guerrilla-held port.

While in dry-dock being repaired, a Mitsubishi medium bomber came carelessly low over the So What. The pilot's curiosity caused him to circle for a better look, during which time the alert gunners on the So What manned the 20-millimeters and, as the plane approached, opened fire and scored direct hits with the first burst. The plane managed to stay in the air for a few miles but came down near guerrilla-held territory and valuable information was secured from the plane as well as from the bodies of the dead crew.

Such examples of courage and success fully justified the efforts which were made to deliver heavier armament to the guerrillas.

One interesting idea which didn't work out was the one which occurred to Chick in one of his trips by sailboat—that of the bazooka, which because of its peculiar characteristics he thought might assist the guerrillas in combating the enemy patrol boats and would make it possible to arm each supply boat, so as to permit them to sail without escort.

Such examples of courage and success with crude weapons made Chick redouble his efforts to secure heavier armament for the guerrillas. Presently he got the idea that the bazooka might assist the guerrillas in engaging the enemy, and might even permit them to go out in combat against patrol launches.

"The bazooka has terrific fire power," he explained to Colonel Fertig. "Furthermore it can be hidden in the bottom of an innocent-looking sailboat and brought into play when a Jap launch gets within short range."

"We'll give it a try," said the colonel.

A bazooka was therefore put aboard a small sailboat which proceeded out to look for the enemy. A Jap patrol boat was not long in showing up. When the enemy approached within fifty yards the bazooka was snatched from its hiding place on the deck of the cockpit and brought into play. Several Japs were killed, the launch was set on fire, and the guerrillas were jubilant.

This glee was short-lived, however. The crippled launch managed to get away—and spread the news. Thereafter the Japanese took no chances and started to fire on guerrilla sailboats immediately they came into range.

"The bazooka," Chick was forced to confess, "actually backfired on the guerrillas, though it was used with good effect later against Jap strongholds."

Not all the radio sets which Chick brought in on his second trip were destined for coast-watcher or guerrilla use. A certain portion of each shipment of this equipment was laid aside for civilian use.

In occupied sections, Chick had learned only too well, it was definitely punishable to be caught listening to a short-wave radio. Even the imposition of the death penalty failed to stop clandestine listening, however, so the Japanese called in all radios in occupied areas and made them over into medium-wave sets. This presupposed a range of only fifty miles, due to the peculiar atmospheric conditions in the Philippines, and meant that the listeners could hear only Jap Propaganda broadcasts . . . until General MacArthur approved the plan of sending into the Philippines a considerable number of battery-operated short-wave receivers, which were distributed among the guerrilla areas and the occupied areas. There was a plan set up for delivering to the Manila area a rebroadcast station, which could cover the Manila area by picking up short-wave Allied programs and rebroadcasting them on medium wave. Parsons arranged with Major Anderson on his trip to the Luzon area in August 1944 for a site to be selected, a power unit to be installed, and arrangements made for the maintenance and operation of the set. The actual delivery of the equipment and qualified personnel failed, however, due to enemy interruption, which prevented the submarine making delivery as planned.

Due to the relatively small size of their garrison forces in the south and central sections, the Japanese were not able to maintain vigilance against wildcat radios in the unoccupied areas. However, electricity, as well as radios, was scarce. It required many hours of perspiring pedaling by boys on bicycles, hitched up to generators, to recharge the batteries.

It was necessary, therefore, not only to get added sets to the people but to determine the hour of greatest reception by the most people. Making a survey of the towns and villages, Chick found that five to six was the most favorable hour of the day to reach the largest number of Filipinos.

In Australia General MacArthur had built one of the strongest radio broadcasting stations under our flag. In the fall of 1943, he began to beam daily programs to the Islands at the time found by Commander Parsons to be the hour most suited to the people in the area. And just before here turned to Australia from the maiden trip of the cargo carrier Chick had a chance to witness the reception of this broadcast as it applied to one small town—representative of many.

Word travels fast in a little Filipino barrio. Just before five o'clock, on this December evening in 1943, the entire populace gathered before the house of the leading citizen.

Chick Parsons looked down on the newly scrubbed faces of the farmers back from the fields, the guerrillas in from the trails. He saw the housewives hurrying from their kitchens after the light evening meal, and the little children squatting excitedly in the dust. All eyes centered on the new radio which Chick had set up on the porch of the mayor. All ears listened as he said:

"Amigos, you have asked me when the Aid is coming. You have asked me many times. You have been very patient. This," he patted the radio, "is your answer; tonight, tomorrow night, and every night until the Japanese are driven from your lands."

Chick looked at his watch. It was fifteen seconds before five. He turned on the radio.

At five a voice spoke. A voice that every loyal Filipino heard in his dreams.

"This is General Douglas MacArthur," said the voice. "I shall return."

The opening music, which was a familiar method of locating and tuning the station before news started to flow, was the Philippine national anthem. It is noteworthy that this piece was a great morale builder to the people, not only in this little village but all over the Islands—in the mountains, secret spots in houses in Manila, coast-watchers' huts overlooking the sea, guerrilla camps and outposts.

The news followed, in the voice of a reporter speaking English—the language the children had learned in school, the elders understood—the language of promise. News of the day in every theater of war. Especially news of the Southwest Pacific Theater.

Men, women, and children listened, drawing soft breath so as not to miss a word. Guerrilla scribes—peacetime stenographers and secretaries—scribbled furiously. There were no sound effects of combat, but at the side of the people, in their minds' eye, American soldiers, sailors, and Marines fought their way toward the Philippines.

At six o'clock the voice again.

"I shall return."

That was all.

The representatives of the Guerrilla Propaganda Corps hurried off to copy the high lights of the news, place it on remote bulletin boards. Messengers sped over twisting mountain trails to high, lonely villages. The people before the house of the mayor raised their soft voices in a hum of comment and conversation. Tears glistened in their eyes. In the sifting dusk they gathered around Commander Parsons. Now and again a small brown hand crept out and touched him, very gently.

Presently the villagers drifted away to their homes. Twisted bits of wild cotton flickered fitfully in the bowls of coconut oil as they sat and discussed the miracle they had witnessed. Night birds called from the great shadowy trees. It was eight o'clock, bedtime ... in the Philippine Islands. Tonight was different.

Now they could understand why and how it was necessary for General MacArthur to retake the islands to the south of their homeland first. Now they could wait.

Long ago he had promised that he would come back. He had said it again, through the lips of the commander, their friend. He had said it tonight, in person.

"I shall return."

The people let the three words linger on their tongues, like candy. The long-awaited tomorrow did not seem so far away tonight.

Lying on a rough mat in the house of the mayor, his head pillowed on his arm. Chick Parsons smiled. Somewhere offshore, he knew, the submarine waited. Her foreward and after torpedo rooms were empty of all but ammunition. She had delivered her burden of hope to the Filipino people, of arms to their fighting men.

But her first mission was only half done.

In the steel chambers of the submarine sailors laid out blankets for the evacuees. Their tomorrow had come.

CHAPTER XIII

FROM OCTOBER 1943, UNTIL THE INVASION EVERY SPYRON submarine returning to base in the Southwest Pacific evacuated as many American and Allied nationals as possible from the Philippine Islands, including a high percentage of women and children. These evacuations were accomplished under rather difficult circumstances.

On the lower and central islands of the Philippines there were, at the time of the surrender, a number of American servicemen who proved non-adaptable to guerrilla warfare. They were good soldiers, but they had been trained in an entirely different type of encounter and could not lead Filipinos successfully. Likewise in the hills were numbers of American and Allied civilians who, for one reason or another. General MacArthur wished removed from the Islands.

During the first few trips by operational submarine Spyron was able to evacuate only persons of special importance. The addition of a cargo-carrying sub to the Spyron fleet made it possible to step up this process considerably and a definite policy encouraging such evacuations was adopted by General MacArthur's headquarters.

This move on the part of the SWP Headquarters was accelerated by Commander Parsons' reports of the changing attitude of the Japanese toward all American and Allied nationals throughout the Islands. In December 1943, they indicated that their meager tolerance was wearing even thinner. They followed this up, shortly, with a widely disseminated proclamation which read:

The amnesty under which Americans have been guaranteed safety and internment by the Imperial Japanese Government is about to expire. After 25 of January 1944 any American found in the Islands, whether unsurrendered soldier or civilian, will be executed without trial.

Having placed his last radio and delivered his last carbine, Chick Parsons set about securing a full load of human freight for the return to Australia. He therefore hurried to Colonel Fertig's headquarters to try to make contact with the various groups wishing to be removed before the deadline.

"Look at this," said the colonel, and handed Chick a message that had just come in from Peralta's headquarters on Panay.

Report thirteen American nationals, among them women and children, have just been slaughtered by the Japanese on Panay.

"There's no time to waste, is there? The Japs aren't waiting for that deadline," Chick said.

"Their patrols are scouring the countryside with blood in the eye," the colonel added. "They've cut off, for the time being, two groups I've been trying to bring in."

"Who are they?" Chick asked.

"Man named Kohler, his wife, two daughters, and a missionary nurse. Also a Dutch mining engineer, Devries, with his wife and two little boys."

Chick frowned. The enemy was no respecter of American womanhood, he knew. If they captured these women and young girls . . .

"My lads are out now trying to contact Kohler and Devries," said the colonel.

"Good. Keep trying. Now about this Negros group. ...."

"Forty missionaries and their families from the Silliman Institute."

"That's an unwieldy bunch, too conspicuous for my liking. Let me get in touch with Colonel Abcede, and see if he thinks he can get them down to the shore unobserved."

The guerrilla chief of Negros not only thought he could but shortly radioed that he had managed to get this company of men, women, and children to a point of embarkation. "The Japanese are exerting great pressure on me," he added. "Please hurry."

Chick was already on his way by submarine.

While en route the submarine picked up a message from Colonel Fertig, indicating that he had made contact with the two small groups in his territory and awaited orders as to their disposition. Touching briefly at the nearest guerrilla headquarters, Chick dispatched a sailboat with orders to pick up Fertig's evacuees and hurried on toward Negros.

Just off the rendezvous point the radio operator handed Chick another dispatch from Colonel Abcede which had been routed through General MacArthur's headquarters. This message indicated that the Japanese had staged a raid on the rendezvous area and forced the Silliman missionaries up into the hills.

"Seems to be a damned sight easier to land inanimate objects in the Philippines than to take people off," Chick observed to the skipper of the sub. "What do you think, Frank?"

"Well, we're here," said the young captain. "We better surface and have a look."

Just at daybreak the submarine made a submerged reconnaissance and, finding no particular enemy activity in the area, broke surface. A young guerrilla promptly paddled out from shore in a canoe.

"What's the dope?" Chick asked when the boy came within earshot.

"Japanese patrols were here last night," he said. "Gone now."

"And the missionaries?"

The guerrilla lad pointed to the distant hills.

"Do you have radio contact with them?"

"No, Commander."

"How far is it to the hills?"

"Half a day's march."

"Let's go get that Mindanao gang first," said the captain. "There's no sense sitting around here, whistling for a breeze."

Chick looked at the dense jungle. No telling what eyes were watching from the brush.

"Roger," he said.

The submarine started back to Mindanao. Just off the coast Chick received another blow, by radio.

"Sailboat intercepted by the enemy," the message from Colonel Fertig read. "Crew killed and vessel captured. Name new rendezvous point and approximate time of meeting."

Chick groaned.

"Sorry to give you this runaround, Frank."

"You name it, Chick," said the skipper calmly. "We'll get there. I hate to think of American kids falling into the hands of those bastards."

Fertig radioed advice to the sub through the Navy Control Radio Station that he had contacted Lieutenant Colonel Bowler, his chief of staff, who was in the area where these parties were located, and instructed him to have the men, women, and children at any spot on the north coast of Mindanao, in the area available to the parties, and, upon arrival at this rendezvous, to burn two beach fires one hundred yards apart, beginning at midnight.

The Filipinos are great fishermen and in peacetime go out at night with Coleman-type lanterns on the prows of their boats to attract their prey. War, of course, had made impossible the use of gasoline or kerosene, but had not stopped the natives from engaging in their favorite occupation—now a necessity rather than a pleasure. Torches were therefore devised of dried coconut palm leaves and all through the Jap occupation it was not at all uncommon to see fires on the beaches, or just offshore, at night.

As the submarine came within the area where the evacuees would probably be located, Latta and Chick were elated to sight two huge bonfires blazing briskly on the shore. They were so bright that they were first seen at a distance of about ten miles. The sub sailed on the bonfires and made a rough calculation that they were a hundred yards apart. As the submarine approached the shore the prearranged blinker signal by a directional blinking device was flashed in the direction of the bonfires, and shortly after a young Filipino guerrilla officer bobbed alongside in a banca.

"Party ready?" he was asked.

"I'll say. The area is very hot, sir."

Chick was aware of that. The Jap garrison at Cagayan was only a couple of miles away.

"Where's that patrol launch?"

"It's passing up and down on a course between you and the shore about every hour," said the officer.

"Is that the biggest craft you've got hereabouts?" said Chick, looking at the banca, whose capacity was not over six at most.

"Yes sir. There's quite a gang of people on shore and heaps of baggage." The skipper raised his eyebrows.

"Moving day on Mindanao," he remarked.

"I'll take care of that," said Commander Parsons, and stepped into the boat. On the way in he gave instructions to the officer. "You're to take the women and children first, and watch that launch. Don't leave the submarine for a return trip until you get a signal from the captain that the coast is clear."

"No baggage," he informed the evacuees when he reached shore. "Sorry."

Of the four hundred and fifty-odd persons whom Chick Parsons was to take out of the Philippines, it was his later claim that at least four hundred and fifty-one were writing a book. This group was no exception to the rule. The men promptly put up a howl of protest.

"But I've been working for months on a manuscript," one objected.

"And I have all sorts of accounts and diaries that are priceless," said another.

Chick stared at the men in amazement.

"More valuable than the lives of your families, not to mention a crew of about a hundred men and the biggest submarine in the fleet?"

"Well . . ." The men dropped their eyes.

All night long the little boat crept in and out of the bay, dodging Jap patrol boats. Just at dawn Chick came out with the last load, gave a sigh of relief as he felt the Diesels throb beneath him.

The submarine still had an impressive gantlet of planes, destroyers, and launches to run. But death for this handful of American and Allied citizens, if it came, would at least be swift and clean.

"Let's have another whack at Negros," said Chick. Obediently the sub moved out into Mindanao Sea.

Below decks the evacuees were herded into the forward and after torpedo rooms which were to be their homes for the next week or ten days. For the sick and aged a few cots were made available. For the majority, however, a blanket and a bit of deck space was all that was possible in the narrow compartments which the passengers shared with the chief torpedoman and his crew.

"Home was never like this, hey?" said the good-natured chief to a little girl who was staring about in amazement.

"No," said the little miss, "this is more fun."

"Now let's see if we can't rig you and brother here a more shipshape outfit." And the chief set to work with needle and thread to replace the tattered garments of the children.

Everyone slept in his clothes. There was no privacy. No one was permitted to move about except to go to the head.

A rather embarrassed junior officer shortly presented himself to one of the matrons.

"The captain has appointed you master of the head for the women and children. If you'll come with me I'll show you how the plumbing works."

The lady smiled.

"Half an hour aboard submarine and I'm promoted," she said as she followed the officer into the tiny compartment.

"To accomplish a careful and successful flush," said the ensign in a singsong schoolboy voice, "you turn this valve first, then this one. . . ." He demonstrated.

The lady concentrated on the various pressure valves.

"Think you can remember the sequence?" said the officer anxiously.

"I hope so."

"So do the mess attendants."

"What happens if I turn the wrong valve first?"

The ensign chose his words carefully.

"Do you drive a car?" he asked.

"I used to."

"Ever shift into reverse instead of forward?"

Three meals a day were served aboard the submarine. Sometimes four and even five. Since the battery and crew's wardroom could only accommodate eight to ten officers, it was impossible to feed the passengers there. They therefore set up their own mess, offering their services to the cooks as helpers, dishwashers, and kitchen police. The women also assisted in the preparation and serving of food, which was done at times that would not interfere with the operations of the vessel.

"I never thought to see the day," said the veteran cook, "when I'd have a bunch of ladies hoppin' around my galley. This is certainly a very fancy war."

It was still, however, a war.

While cruising submerged, General Quarters was sounded. The chief torpedo man dropped his sewing and stood by his torpedo tubes. The evacuees exchanged glances and drew the children out of the way. But there was no panic. One small voice breathed out in the sudden silence of the forward torpedo compartment.

"What was the bell for, Mama?"

The chief torpedoman winked.

"The skipper is a great fisherman," he said. "I think he's got a bite. Maybe we'll have a nice Jap fish for lunch."

In the conning tower the captain trained his periscope on a small Jap merchantman, steaming slowly in toward the port which they had just left.

"No escort," he told Chick. "The gunners are getting a little rusty. Let's see how much they've forgotten about a 6-inch."

The submarine popped up out of the sea, the gunners leaped to their positions, and in a matter of minutes the Rising Sun on the side of the merchantman was sliding toward the bottom. Her only reply had been a harmless spatter of machine-gun bullets.

The sinking was accomplished in full view of guerrilla soldiers crowding the shores, and to the accompaniment of their lusty cheers.

"I have a hunch," said Chick, watching the survivors bobbing shoreward, "that those boys are going to catch ...malaria."

Enemy interference blocked the second attempt of the submarine to contact the missionary group on Negros. Only on the third try was the attempt successful—and this success, as well as that of all the missions attempted by submarine, Commander Parsons ascribed wholly to the skipper of the submarine.

It must be stated that this kind of duty, approaching strange shores patrolled by enemy craft of all types, requires a higher type of bravery than is needed for regular war patrols—which takes guts enough. Yet all these skippers have responded beautifully to the challenge of these trips. They have considered it a job to be done and they have done it magnificently in a manner fully recognized by General MacArthur and Presidents Quezon and Osmena.

CHAPTER XIV

IT WAS NOT AT ALL UNUSUAL FOR SPYRON SUBMARINES to launch and receive attacks with evacuees aboard. While doubtless they felt fear, the behavior of these passengers was perfect. They co-operated beautifully, did not show panic, nor interfere with the work of the men. And the children universally took it all as a grand lark.

Commander Parsons' many harrowing experiences have not succeeded in making him hard-boiled. Among the many warm spots in his heart, children occupy an especially favored place.

Back in happier days in Manila, Chick's two oldest boys came running into the house one morning, complaining tearfully, "Every kid in Manila has an Uncle Chick except us."

"Okay," replied their father. "I'll be Uncle Chick to you too." And this is what his children, along with hundreds of other youngsters, call him today.

It is not strange, then, that of the many evacuees Chick Parsons has carried to safety his favorite is a child—young Stevie Crytser, aged about three at the time Chick picked him up. When war broke out Bob Crytser, a former associate of Chick's in the Luzon Stevedoring Company, was working in the port director's office at Davao in a civilian capacity. The bombing of Mindanao's great port coincided with that of Pearl Harbor. For safety, Crytser sent his wife Glenda and their small baby to a hemp plantation outside the city.

Davao fell swiftly after Pearl Harbor, and Bob was interned. Glenda, finding herself in proximity to a Jap civilian community, took little Stevie to the hills of Mindanao. Pressure from the enemy became stronger and stronger, forcing the young mother and infant back into the wilds until they found themselves completely cut off from their accustomed foods.

There was nothing in Glenda Crytser's baby manual to meet such a crisis and no other alternative but to fall back on the menu of the hill people and their children—boiled, unpolished rice and bananas.

This was Stevie's entire diet for two whole years.

When Commander Parsons first saw Stevie the little boy was seated on the knee of a torpedoman, clad in a fragment of cloth—the healthiest-looking youngster alive. In his hand he held the first piece of bread he had ever seen.

"What is it?" he inquired in bewilderment.

"Food," said the sailor. "Good to eat. Put it in your mouth."

Stevie promptly obeyed. He chewed thoughtfully for a moment. Then he wrinkled his tiny nose in disgust and spat.

"I want a banana," he said decisively.

Chick looked at Glenda Crytser, who hadn't fared so well, physically, as her son. "That's all he's been eating, Chick, bananas and a little rice. I don't know how ordinary food is going to affect him."

Commander Parsons gave a brief order. Presently three large stalks of bananas were dumped on the deck of the submarine. Stevie's eyes gleamed.

"Mmmm," he said, and popped one into his mouth.

Ordinarily the evacuees were forced to remain in their compartments and were not allowed to wander about or group on deck—in fact they never knew whether the submarine was upon or below the surface. Air conditioning, however, rendered this no hardship.

Stevie was the exception to a lot of rules. He was accustomed to an active life, did not care where he was going or with whom, so long as he was going somewhere. He promptly took over the ship, much to the delight of the crew, to whom the presence of women and children was a welcome novelty.

Stevie, in Chick's estimation, probably knows more about a submarine than any person alive.

One afternoon, however, the little fellow was missing. The ship was searched from stem to stern. A submarine does not have unlimited possibilities for concealment.

No Stevie, however.

Finally Chick, passing through the crews' quarters, had a hunch. In one of the upper bunks snoozed a veteran of a hundred underwater encounters with the enemy. On the inside of the bunk, half concealed by a hairy arm which bore tattooed evidence of quite another type of encounter, lay Stevie.

Though he was sound asleep, one small fist still clutched a half-eaten banana.

The presence of the evacuees aboard proved both a diversion and a morale builder. The crew shared their clothing and cigarettes with the men, did everything possible for the women, and were especially fond of the children. Sailors vied with each other in stitching up snappy nautical outfits for their favorites and by the time the submarine reached the mainland of Australia the youngsters were as neatly turned out as any gob on shore leave.

Naturally when depth charges started to rain down and jar the submarine, or when the cargo carrier was attacking a surface target, the evacuees felt some anxiety. They would probably, in Chick's words, "have preferred to take their chances ashore with the Japs." However, while uncertain what was going on, they did not become upset but rather expressed the greatest confidence in captain and crew by remaining quietly in their places.

The kids actually shrieked with glee when the depth bombs exploded and cried: "Boy, we sure nearly got 'em that time."

"Many of them," Chick concluded, "mistook Jap depth charges for our torpedoes, unaware that in many cases only a matter of feet stood between them and destruction. Nature is kind to children in this way, as I know from watching the reaction of my own youngsters to situations which Katsy and I found terrifying and horrible."

With the arrival of the submarine in Australia, the busy naval base opened its eyes in amazement at the crowd of men, women, and children climbing up out of the hatches. The generosity of the crew was evident. Each evacuee wore at least one article of Navy issue and the children were completely decked out in full uniform.

"Parsons," said one officer, "seems to be recruiting midgets."

The evacuees, blinking at the bright sun—and with the tears that came to their eyes when they realized they had at last found sanctuary—breathed in the free air of the Commonwealth as though they could not get enough. For a moment some of them looked as though they might collapse.

Then the physicians and nurses General MacArthur had sent, the Red Cross girls with clothing and comfort kits surrounded the group. Under the aegis of their new caretakers, the evacuees were quickly loaded aboard big Army transport planes and taken to a rest home which the American Red Cross, at the general's request, had set up at one of the summer resorts near Brisbane.

A great many of the refugees were emaciated, all were undernourished and quite out of touch with civilized life. A period of a month or so was allotted to permit them to regain their physical health and mental equilibrium, for the strain on most had been long and hard. Then they were sent home.

Chick Parsons drew a sigh of relief when he had finally discharged his obligation and returned the cargo carrier safely to Commodore Haines.

"How do you feel, Chick?" asked the commodore, who had met Commander Parsons at the dock.

"Like a father who has married off his last homely daughter," said Chick. "What's new?"

From the commodore it was learned that the sister ship of the one Chick had just stepped from had been assigned to Spyron service and would be expected on station in the near future.

President Quezon, he explained, had personally gone to bat for the guerrillas—and Spyron—with President Roosevelt in Washington. He had argued that the more medicines the Filipinos were able to receive, the better their ability to resist the enemy; the more carbines, the greater the fighting strength of the guerrillas at invasion time.

President Quezon had not lacked statistics to back up his arguments, for he had been following Parsons' progress with the greatest of interest and satisfaction. It had not been difficult to sell the Commander in Chief of the Army and Navy on Spyron's accomplishments and potentialities.

"This second cargo carrier is the result," the commodore concluded. "You're the father of twins, Chick. What do you say to that?"

Chick Parsons thought of the hopeful little faces of the Filipinos. He felt the touch of their small brown hands. For once he could not answer.

No longer could Commander Parsons call himself a "skipper without a ship"—for Spyron had become a fleet. To the two largest cargo-carrying subs in United States service Commodore Haines added other units as time went on and they could be spared from operational duties.

In this manner did the Navy demonstrate how completely sold it was on Spyron, its purpose, and its leader. The Army, represented by Colonel Whitney, exhibited a like confidence. A steady stream of arms, ammunition, signal equipment, and personnel flowed into the Philippine Islands, first from Australian bases—then, as American forces marched irresistibly through New Guinea, from bases there.

Chick and his small organization labored like titans, fighting the clock to assure every guerrilla of a carbine, every important observation post of a radio and staff by invasion time.

By spring of 1944, Chick had the satisfaction of knowing that Spyron was steadily reaching both these goals, while the expenditure of firepower in guerrilla ranks had been met. It was only necessary now to build up reserves of ammunition to take care of any demand that the guerrillas might be expected to put upon the supply at invasion, and to include heavier armament.

In the occupied areas the spy ring increased its effectiveness, extending its membership to include even puppets of whom the Japanese felt so sure that they dressed them in Jap uniforms. And American counter-propaganda hammered a single phrase unceasingly into the minds of Jap and Filipino alike.

In addition to his daily radio broadcasts General MacArthur published a monthly magazine, in English, called Free Philippines. This newssheet, containing pictorial reporting of the war on all fronts and a detailed accounting of progress in the Pacific, was brought into the Islands regularly by Chick and his men, and given wide distribution.

Free Philippines had an irritatingly persistent way of popping up on the tables of Jap garrison commanders, the desks of puppet officials in Manila—to haunt them with the locked flags of the United States and the Commonwealth on the cover. To dog their dreams with the simple line at the bottom: "I shall return. MacArthur."

There could no longer be any doubt in the mind of Jap, puppet, and people alike that the day of reckoning was approaching.

In August 1944 the Japanese boasted in press and radio that a group of guerrillas, including "the notorious Chick Parsons," had been captured and executed.

Four days after this news had been picked up by the American press Katsy Parsons received a radio reading:

PAY NO ATTENTION TO JAPANESE WISHFUL THINKING.
THE REWARD FOR PARSONS IS STILL UNCLAIMED.
(Signed) Chico

CHAPTER XV

THERE WERE A NUMBER OF POINTS IN CONNECTION WITH the proposed landing of United States forces in Leyte which could only be handled by personal contact.

In October 1944 Chick Parsons returned to New Guinea after a final briefing of the guerrilla movement in the Philippine Islands.

A trip into the area east of Manila, on which he was accompanied by a young naval officer, Larry Sinclair, and the son of Colonel Whitney, Private Courtney Whitney, assured him that the Intelligence network in the occupied section was functioning properly. The ether above the Islands was full of guerrilla code and Chick could count over a hundred coast-watcher radio stations on twenty-four-hour operation. In the hands of every guerrilla-soldier gleamed a carbine, rifle, or tommy gun, and ammunition lay piled in the hills against all possible present and future needs.

Spyron had made its deadline. A miracle had been accomplished in a few short months. The guerrillas were ready for the test.

Summoned to the headquarters of Lieutenant General Walter Krueger's Sixth Army in Hollandia, Chick Parsons found himself in the midst of an extremely solemn conclave of staff officers.

"We have sent for you, Commander Parsons," said the general slowly, "because you have been so vitally responsible for the development of the free movement in the Philippines, and particularly because you know the terrain and the people of Leyte so thoroughly."

"Leyte?" Chick's eyes opened wide.

"The Sixth Army will invade Leyte on or about October 20."

Chick drew a deep breath. "This is it," he said, "at last."

"This is it," said the general.

It was also the first intimation to Commander Parsons that General MacArthur had decided to bypass Mindanao for Leyte in the midst of the Visayan group farther north. The strategy, Chick immediately saw, was both daring and brilliant. Everyone, Jap and guerrilla alike, presumed that the Americans would land on the south coast of Mindanao, either around Davao or the Ilana Bay region west of Cotabato, where the island pinches together—giving easy ten-mile access to the north coastal road. For the past month, the guerrilla network had reported intense enemy concentrations in this region and the arrival of troop reinforcements, big coastal guns, and aircraft, in impressive quantities.

Had there been no means of concentrating and controlling enemy forces on Mindanao, it was pointed out, a landing would have to be made on that island either first or at the same time as on Leyte. The availability of this means in the form of thirty thousand guerrillas was a tribute to the efforts of Colonel Whitney, Colonel Fertig, and Spyron.

"There are, however," General Krueger continued, "various problems in connection with this proposed landing in Leyte which are peculiar to the Philippines and which make this invasion different from any so far attempted in the Pacific."

A landing in Leyte would be a landing in thoroughly Americanized and friendly territory so far as the inhabitants were concerned. In the fulfillment of his great ambition and long-standing promise General MacArthur was extremely anxious not to bring death and destruction to the Filipino people under the banner of deliverance. Both the general and President Osmena were determined that every possible precaution be taken to spare the civilian populace.

"How to remove loyal Filipinos out of the various areas to be attacked without giving advance information to the enemy is something else again," continued General Krueger. "Likewise how to co-ordinate Colonel Kangleon's troops with our own, without revealing exact invasion plans."

For security reasons General MacArthur's staff dared not entrust the accomplishment of these aims even to radio code. The possibility of sending an advance party from Sixth Army ahead of the troops had been considered—and discarded. Such a party would only be a walking advertisement of invasion.

"Besides," General Krueger added, "if any emissary with full cognizance of invasion plans were to be captured and forced to give the show away—it would be disastrous. The lives of thousands of American and Filipino boys are at stake."

The room grew still. The staff worried this problem in their minds as they had worried it for days—without solution.

Chick Parsons' voice broke the silence at last. "I don't see any way to accomplish these objectives," he said softly, "except for me to go in ahead of the troops."

"You?"

"I ought to be qualified by now."

The staff had not thought of Commander Parsons for this mission. In fact on no prior landing had anyone, in full awareness of the complete plan of operation, been sent in ahead of the first wave.

"You're quite aware of what you would be up against, Commander?" Chick was asked.

Chick nodded.

"How would you get into the Islands unobserved?" inquired General Krueger after a significant pause. "By submarine?"

Chick knew that Surigao Strait, the logical entrance to Leyte, was heavily mined against access of any surface or underseas craft to Leyte Gulf.

Besides, from the most advantageous landing point by submarine to Colonel Kangleon's present guerrilla headquarters would be a good ten days' hike. By the time Chick had navigated the jungle trails the bombings would have started, the fleet would be underway.

"I'd have to be dropped by plane," he decided.

"Can you sell the commander of the Seventh Fleet on that proposition?"

"I can try," said Chick simply. He bent forward, his dark face suddenly full of eagerness. The invasion would be the culmination of all his efforts, the supreme test of Chick's belief in the guerrilla-soldiers of the Philippines. It must have every chance of success. "What do you say, sir?"

"The man really wants to go," a staff member murmured in amazement.

"Of course," said Chick. "You wouldn't expect me to warm the bench on the day of the big game, would you?"

The general gave his support to the idea, which later was developed and approved by General Sutherland and General MacArthur.

Vice-Admiral Klinkaid, commander of the Seventh Fleet, admitted Commander Parsons to audience—and objection. He was not at all sure that such a plan could be carried out successfully. Chick would have to go by Catalina Black Cat, an amphibious plane, slow and extremely vulnerable to anything else that flew. The admiral thought it extremely inadvisable to risk valuable Navy equipment and even more valuable trained personnel on such a hair-raising mission.

Then he let Commander Parsons talk.

Within a matter of hours Chick was climbing aboard the flagship of Admiral Wagner, air officer of the Seventh Fleet, a letter from Admiral Kinkaid in hand.

What Admiral Wagner said to the request to authorize the squadron commander of the Catalina Black Cats to lineup a special crew and plane— "Destination to be designated by the above-named Parsons, Charles, Commander, USNR"—is unrecorded. Chick got his plane.

On the ninth of October Commander Parsons hurried back to Hollandia for last-minute instructions from General Richard K. Sutherland, MacArthur's chief of staff.

The Navy felt that Chick himself could secure the specialized intelligence needed. The Army on the other hand believed that one of their own Intelligence officers could better gather the information General Krueger required and send it out in the form most acceptable to him and his staff.

"Lieutenant Colonel Frank Rawolle of Army Intelligence will accompany you," said General Sutherland.

"Fine," said Chick. "Frank will be a great help. Besides, I've got quite a few chores to do as is."

It was of primary importance to persuade the people in attack areas to take to the hills: and even more important to prevent them from coming down and falling on the necks of the invading forces, as they well might do in their enthusiasm and relief.

General Sutherland had had leaflets prepared in the States and flown out by special air courier. These would be given to every soldier, stressing the use of the greatest discretion and care, on Dog Day, where civilians were concerned.

"Nevertheless I'm not counting too heavily on these pamphlets to enable a bunch of jittery GIs to distinguish between friend and foe when they hit the beach," warned the general.

It was not expected that the Japs would be able to withstand the tons of hot iron and steel which the Navy and Air Wing were grimly preparing for Japanese garrisons. It was essential therefore that Colonel Kangleon have every possible guerrilla-soldier ambushed along all anticipated retreat and withdrawal trails.

Furthermore, the staff wished the guerrilla network to pinpoint enemy positions, the disposition and movement of enemy troops, hour by hour, as the invading forces drew near.

"You will be expected to supervise the screening and evaluation of this information. The fleet will also require general information as to enemy strength and disposition on the entire island of Leyte."

These were Chick's major missions. In his "spare time" there were a few other "chores" requiring his attention. He must contact Lieutenant Colonel Smith on Samar to line up his forces in coordination with anticipated Army forays into that island. He must secure from guerrilla sources information of enemy placement in Surigao at the northern end of Mindanao and in and around the vital strait through which the fleet must pass. Finally he must line up "employees" for use after the landing on D-Day.

All this Commander Parsons must do—and not get captured.

"The Japs," the general stated, "are experts in the Machiavellian art of securing information from prisoners by torture. You know something about that."

"Yes."

"They also use a serum or drug which neutralizes the will of even the strongest character. In order to perform your missions successfully and to be sure that the enemy doesn't get information about our plans, this is one time you definitely must not be captured."

"I won't be," said Chick firmly.

By way of preparation for his trip Commander Parsons took off his Navy uniform, put on a pair of shorts, a ragged shirt, and moccasins. He then regarded the somewhat elaborate equipment of his companion with amusement and tolerance. For Lieutenant Colonel Rawolle was taking carbine, ammunition, sidearms, canteen, and other items which he had found essential on his previous expeditions.

"Ready?" said Chick at last.

"Sure," said Frank. "How about you?"

"Let's go. The plane's waiting."

The Army officer gave Chick a quick up-and-down.

"Aren't you going to take a carbine?"

Chick shook his head.

"Not even a sidearm?"

"Frank, I have landed in the Philippines enough times to realize that mobility has proven much more successful than lugging a firearm. This is especially true in the Philippines where you can count on the majority of people being friendly. I realize that on your reconnaissance and scouting expeditions down in New Guinea you ran a terrific risk of discovery and capture due to the fact that most of the natives could be considered unfriendly. Actually here in the Philippines I have treated my various landings almost as if I were landing on the coast of California."

"I'll continue to carry my carbine. It's not easy for me to realize the changed conditions here from the experiences in Guinea."

At eight o'clock on the night of October 11, a Catalina flying boat trundled over the surface of the bay at an advanced Navy base. It bounced heavily into the air and headed for Leyte.

The interior of the plane was not as hot as the sweat on Commander Parsons' brow indicated. It was not the sweat of fear, however. The malaria he had contracted long ago was asserting itself again.

River stay away from my door, Chick thought, and added the prayer—just nine days more anyhow.

CHAPTER XVI

WE HAD TO TAKE TWO SHOTS AT LEYTE BEFORE WE SCORED A HIT.
The afternoon of the eleventh Chick had spent aboard the flagship at
the Black Cat base going over the course minutely with Pilot Shinn and his copilot, charting all information in his possession about places where the Japs
were known to have spotters, radio stations, and radar. The crew had been
kept to a minimum of two pilots, navigator, radio operator, mechanic, and
two enlisted men, to render the party less conspicuous should the plane be
forced down and a hike to guerrilla territory be indicated.

Four hours had been allowed to enable Chick and Frank Rawolle to
reach one of three alternate destinations. They were counting on the darkness
of midnight to enable them to land unobserved and contact friendly guerrillas.

For the first two hours a quarter-moon guided their course. Then fleecy
clouds began to obscure this faint light. Finally the moon disappeared entirely
and a spatter of rain scratched the surface of the glass porthole out of which
the men were anxiously peering.

Over Leyte proper they encountered rain squalls. Mist shrouded the
plane completely. Lightning danced like neon along the radio antenna and
the pilot called over interphone:

"Any idea where we are, Commander?"

"In one hell of a storm over Leyte somewhere," said Chick. "Can you get
below?"

"Looks like a zero ceiling, but I'll take a chance if you will."

"You're handling the stick. How's the gas?"

"Okay, for the present."

Frantically the plane whirled and circled, seeking a hole in the thick cot-
tony ceiling. The minutes ticked by into hours. There was no slightest letup in
the storm.

"We can't keep this up indefinitely," said Chick's companion nervously,
and presently the pilot called again.

"I'd keep her up here until hell freezes over, Commander, but we've got
just enough gas to get back to base."

"Let's go home then," Chick said reluctantly.

No one said very much on the way back.

In the bright light of morning a small boat bobbed out with a case of
beer for the crew, who were presumed to be returning from the successful ac-
complishment of a difficult mission.

"The two deadheads are still aboard, however," said Chick sadly.

Pilot Shinn looked at his tired crew and passengers.

"Beer is beer," he said.

They took the brew over to a nearby island and silently drank it.

Chick had previously sent a message to Colonel Kangleon, requesting that the leader meet him on the east coast of Leyte Gulf. Reporting to the flagship, he was handed a message which had arrived from Colonel Whitney just after their takeoff. Chick read:

Kangleon on west coast. Does not believe he can get across for several days, due to heavy enemy interference. Recommend your trip be delayed as long as possible.

Chick had no desire to go into a place where he would more or less have to become a guerrilla leader and handle troops. He wanted Kangleon there to take over, for he had too many other duties to perform. Time was extremely short. One day had been lost already and the first bombs were scheduled to fall in just four days.

The captain of the flagship looked at Chick inquiringly.

"I guess we better shove off anyway, whenever your men are ready," Chick decided.

"We'll get you a new crew. Shinn insists on going along as copilot. He's determined to complete his mission successfully."

"Good boy," Chick applauded. "Nobody can say he didn't try."

A couple of hours' rest. A hot luncheon—the last good meal Chick and Colonel Rawolle were to enjoy until D-Day—and the plane took off with a new crew under Pilot Nelson.

Daylight was the chief enemy now.

To avoid detection Captain Nelson flew the plane about six feet above the water the entire distance, and on a course thirty miles east of the Islands, calculated to clear visual posts and radar stations. Then he turned the plane in a half circle.

"Here we go," he said over interphone. "Squeeze the left one."

Just ahead lay the gantlet between Dinagat and Homonhon islands, opposite the entrance to Surigao Strait. On both islands, Chick knew, were Jap radar stations. Their proposed landing was forty miles farther on, up the east coast of Leyte.

The plane must get in, drop the two officers, and get out again before opposition could come from Tacloban Airfield, a matter of minutes by air.

It was unthinkable that they should not be noticed. Their faces grim, the two enlisted men fingered their machineguns.

Dropping the plane even closer to the water, the pilot skimmed it through the narrow passage between Dinagat and Homonhon like a frightened flying fish. The headlands on both sides loomed above them. Then they were through and Leyte just ahead.

Chick beckoned Frank Rawolle and the crew. They gathered around one of the machine-gun blisters.

"The minute she hits," he explained, "we've got to throw out the rubber boat, toss in our gear, and get away. Let's give it a dry run."

They went through the motions of this maneuver until each man knew exactly what was expected of him.

The pilot lifted the plane, slightly, to clear a small fleet of fishing boats. The faces of the natives flashed open mouthed beneath them and were gone. On shore other figures could be seen running for the brush.

"Must think we're a Jap," Chick muttered.

The voice of the pilot, tight with strain, spoke through interphone.

"Stand by for landing," he said.

The Black Cat settled lower. Little waves reached up and ran their hands over her smooth bottom. They felt the yielding of the hull as the pilot tried the surface, lifted the ailerons a fraction, tried again. The Catalina settled. The crunching crash of moving water became an unbroken sound.

Involuntarily Chick glanced at his wrist watch. Four-thirty.

"Now," he said.

With the plane still taxiing, they pitched the rubber boat overboard, tossed in their gear. The two men went through the blister port head first and tumbled in a heap on the bottom of the boat.

A wet rope slapped Chick across the face. The tail fins swam overhead. The two motors picked up with a roar. By the time they had untangled themselves the Black Cat was a speck in the distance.

Chick looked at his watch again. The whole launching had been accomplished in just under a minute.

Once on their own, the different landing techniques customarily employed by the two men came to grips. Rawolle had always heretofore worked in belligerent territory, while Chick's missions had been carried out in what he always expected to be friendly territory. Dusk was settling over the bay, and it was Chick's idea to paddle fast and reach land before shore patrols should come out from Tacloban. Frank, however, was all for drifting around waiting for darkness to insure a landing undetected from shore, assuming that every shadow was a Jap sentry.

Arguing the merits of their varied immediate aims, the two men went around in circles, until Chick finally prevailed sufficiently to maneuver the craft in to a coral shelf running out from the beach. Here Frank Rawolle stated his firm intention of sitting until complete darkness fell.

"Look," he said suddenly, and pointed to a light moving on the shore.

Chick always presumed that anyone he met would be a friend. He promptly yelled: "Barotor."

"Quiet, you idiot," whispered Frank. "He might be a Jap."

Chick paid no attention but repeated the call. A baroto is a small Filipino outrigger. To hail a person on shore in this manner meant, "Come out with a boat and bring me in."

"It never fails," Chick remarked when he had explained this.

The light vanished in the underbrush.

Frank sniffed. "Exception noted."

"It was a native all right. He probably saw the plane come in and thinks we're Japs. I better go in and rouse somebody out. We'll never get this rubber boat over the coral without a puncture."

Chick stepped out into the waist-deep water. His eye fell on his companion's carbine and he warned: "No matter what happens, Frank, don't click the bolt of that carbine. Any guerrilla hearing that sound fires first and challenges afterward."

"I hope you know what you're talking about," said the Army officer.

"I'm really not careless about these things," Chick said. "I just happen to savvy guerrillas pretty well." He began to swim and wade over the sharp coral heads toward shore. Halfway in, Chick turned to look back toward the boat and his companion.

To his alarm, he saw the shadowy figures of a couple of men in a native canoe, apparently sneaking around the reef outside the boat. And suddenly, across the still surface of the cove, came the unmistakable click of a rifle being cocked.

"Oh, my God," Chick whispered and, regardless of coral heads or sea-urchin spines, floundered as quickly as he could back toward the boat, expecting to hear a burst of fire at any time. He found Frank grappling frantically around the shallow bottom.

"Released the cartridge clip instead of the safety, dammitall," he protested. "Whole thing went overboard. Give me a hand here. Chick. Those guys in the canoe will be on us any minute."

Chick looked at the two men who had stopped paddling their banca and were staring at them in what was apparently curiosity and fear.

"Mabuhay," he called.

"Mabuhay," came the uncertain answer.

"Amigos Americanos," said Chick. "We're American friends. And you?"

"Amigos! Amigos!" cried the natives, relief and joy in their voices.

The two native fishermen, for so they proved to be, paddled the officers and their equipment through familiar passages between the coral heads to the beach.

"Leyte," said Chick softly as he felt the sand beneath his bare feet.

"Praise God," echoed Frank Rawolle.

From the small reception committee that had gathered onshore an old Filipino farmer stepped forward and identified himself as a mess attendant at Cavite, now in retirement. This friend offered the hospitality of his small shack, and turned his wife and children to preparing the best meal the circumstances afforded. The entire population of the small village crowded into the little room and watched with pleasure as Chick and Frank devoured the food.

Exhausted by the strain of their experience, the two men immediately dropped off to sleep beneath the watchful eyes of the natives. In the morning the group—as was the custom when important visitors came to a small Filipino town—was still there, maintaining an interested and silent vigil. Two newcomers had also added themselves to the gallery.

"You are guerrilla, no?" Chick inquired, noting the new khaki uniforms, garrison caps, and jungle boots of the men.

They informed Commander Parsons that they had captured a Japanese launch two weeks before and were removing it to an area of greater safety.

"We heard of the arrival of a mysterious plane and came to investigate."

"Good. We're American officers from General MacArthur's headquarters. Will you give us a lift?"

"Anywhere."

Spared a five-mile struggle through the jungle, Chick and Frank Rawolle made their way down the coast aboard the launch, to a trail which led inland to one of Colonel Kangleon's radio stations. Scrambling up this difficult path, they contacted the secret group and Chick made use of the radio. The Navy had given him a codebook and decoding machine. He now sent out his first message, the first of hundreds that would bear his name in the next week. He radioed Southwest Pacific Headquarters:

Party arrived safely.
Parsons.

Next Chick contacted Colonel Kangleon by code and sent the launch to pick up the guerrilla leader of Leyte. Then he sat down to think up a story, for not even Kangleon was all and sent know the exact plan of invasion.

The Japanese, Chick was aware, at this time were reinforcing their garrisons all over the southern and central islands. They had increased their Leyte strength to a total of twenty-four thousand, spread over a large area, conceiving this island as the next logical objective to Mindanao.

With this as a cue. Chick, on Kangleon's arrival, began:

"In just a few days, Colonel, American planes will be striking at all places where the Japanese have strong positions, Leyte included. It is essential that civilians be evacuated from these areas prior to the bombings."

The colonel nodded. "And when do the bombings start, Commander?"

Chick hesitated, but only briefly. He decided it would lend verity to the need for general evacuations if he told the truth on this particular point.

"The bombings will start on the sixteenth and will last a week. The scale will be unprecedented and the bombs will include blockbusters capable of killing all the people in a rather large area. You must tell the people not only to seek safety in the hills but to remain under cover until instructed to return. It is impossible to say when the danger will be over and the bombings finished."

Colonel Kangleon accepted these orders without suspicion or question.

"It shall be done," he said.

"The Japanese," Chick continued, "will not be able to withstand the terrific bombings that will fall upon their garrisons and positions. You know where these are located. Round up every possible guerrilla and surround all retreat routes. Can you do all this in three days?"

"We are ready," said the old colonel quietly.

"Good," said Chick. "Now about the radio network schedules . . ."

They bent their heads to the task of alerting the eyes and ears of the guerrilla forces of Leyte.

On October 16, 1944, the vengeance of free men darkened the skies over the Philippine Islands and the curtain rose on invasion.

CHAPTER XVII

AMERICAN FORCES LANDING ON LEYTE POSSESSED THE MOST complete and extensive information of any that ever invaded an enemy-held area. This was entirely due to the loyalty and good work of the guerrilla-soldiers and their communications system.

On the sixteenth, seventeenth, eighteenth, and nineteenth of October 1944 an endless stream of American bombers blasted the Japanese from one end of Leyte to the other. Up to Samar, across to Negros and Cebu, down to Mindanao the planes shuttled, maintaining twenty-four-hour schedules of destruction.

On the morning of the twentieth one of the greatest armadas in history steamed into Leyte Gulf. In arcs of fire through the early dawn the big guns of the United States fleet pointed out to the Jap the error of his calculations by pulverizing every beach on the east coast from Tacloban south.

Then the soldiers of the Sixth Army climbed down the nets. The landing craft streaked for the beaches. General Douglas MacArthur returned.

Later that morning Commander Parsons and Colonel Kangleon, with a guard of guerrillas, sat on the ruined beach below Tacloban, awaiting transportation to the flagship of the fleet. They were taking a brief respite from their work, and they had done this work well.

Safely in the hills, the people of Leyte watched the bombardment with tears of joy streaming down their cheeks and prayers of relief and gratitude on their lips. Ambushed along the trails, the hearts of guerrilla-soldiers sang as their carbines, rifles, and hand grenades took an ever-mounting toll of the terrified Japanese, fleeing from the wrath that had fallen on their garrisons and coastal defenses. Guerrilla eyes watched everywhere, and wherever the enemy sought sanctuary guerrilla radios reported his whereabouts to the fleet and air arm.

There was no hiding place for the Japanese in the length and breadth of Leyte, except in death.

This was H-Hour, D-Day—for General MacArthur's foresight, for the unceasing endeavor of Commander Parsons, Colonel Kangleon, and Spyron, and for the unconquerable spirit of Filipino guerrilla and unsurrendered American soldier alike.

As soon as he arrived in Leyte on the thirteenth. Chick had arranged with Colonel Kangleon to have all radio stations on the island stand by daily, every hour on the hour.

Messages would then go out from the colonel's control station and each small post would report back with information regarding the Japanese in its particular area. As the fleet approached messages were broadcast from the central station on Leyte at a certain time of day, designated so that all the ships could listen.

Each outgoing message bore the earmark—Parsons.

"Who in hell is this guy Parsons around here anyway?" was the universal question in the fleet. "He seems to be fighting the battle of Leyte single-handed."

So secretly had Chick and his organization functioned, so successfully had they hidden their operations even from brother officers, that until the actual invasion none but a few top staff members knew of the existence of Commander Parsons and Spyron.

They learned on D-Day, however.

Frank Rawolle's messages to the Sixth Army also filled the air, giving rise to Chick's comment: "Parsons and Rawolle seemed to be much in evidence."

From the very first General MacArthur's staff had charted with the utmost care the movements and positions of both Chick and Frank. Their messages were painstakingly analyzed for any indication that they might have fallen into enemy hands. Had this happened, the entire plan of invasion might have had to be changed.

"We did have a couple of scares from patrols," Chick confessed.

One morning, shortly before invasion. Chick was trotting along a mountain trail which paralleled and sometimes crossed the paved sea road. With him, and similarly dressed as local farmers, were two guerrilla guides. Chick, as usual, was unarmed.

Employing his usual security procedure. Chick sent the two guerrillas on ahead to avoid meeting a Jap patrol at one of the cross trails. At such an intersection he observed the guides halt and engage in conversation.

Commander Parsons' mind was full of the many duties he had agreed to perform. A glance at the casual stance of his guides indicated that the coast was clear. Down the trail he pattered, barefooted—and ran right into a Jap patrol.

Chick had no prearranged plan of what he would do in such an emergency, since his whole policy had been to avoid a head-on collision with the Japs. He had come close to the enemy before, but never this close—and never in mental possession of such vital information as the complete plan of invasion.

Petrified with fear, not only for himself but for the possible failure of his mission. Chick could only stand, one hand on the shoulder of a companion, completing a tableau of three innocent natives in conversation.

Rifles slung over their shoulders, shirts open and helmets pushed back on their heads, eighteen Japanese soldiers slogged slowly by. They were so close that Chick could easily have reached out and touched each one. It seemed impossible that at least one of them would not look up and recognize the Caucasian face beneath the straw hat and deep sunburn.

Intent only on their destination, the patrol moved on. The back of the last man disappeared beyond a rise. The clink of their equipment died away.

"Whew!" breathed Chick.

Nature really smiled on me that day by so paralyzing my mind and muscles that I did the only thing possible to save my life—nothing. On another occasion Frank and I were much nearer danger than we knew, but nothing happened and the results proved the risk worthwhile.

How much of the information that went out to the fleet was gathered by Chick's personal reconnaissance he would not say. To the guerrillas, Commander Parsons gives full credit for the success of his undertaking and the boundless aid which the jungle fighters gave United States forces.

For guerrilla agents were everywhere. In the hills, pinpointing artillery positions. On the headlands, in the jungles, along the airstrips, feeding every possible kind of information through their small portable sets into the control stations.

"The Japanese commander at Tacloban has just moved his headquarters to the airfield," came one report—and before the enemy colonel could set up his papers American dive bombers were swooping down.

"Twenty-seven enemy tanks have moved from one end of the Burauen airstrip to the other," flashed a guerrilla observer—and a squadron moved off the decks of the carriers and headed for the kill.

"Forty-man Jap patrol has just left Dulag and is proceeding toward the hills. . . ." Guerrilla carbines were leveled in the tunnels of the jungle.

By nightfall of D-Day five thousand Japanese had found the ultimate and only sanctuary open to them on Leyte, their passing noted only by a fresh scratch on a guerrilla gun butt.

"I did the heavy looking on," said Chick of his activities on and immediately prior to D-Day.

Despite this understatement, Commander Parsons analyzed information at Colonel Kangleon's control station, gave it evaluation, and sent it out in code to the fleet. He dispatched runners in all directions and "screened" their findings. He interviewed agents from Jap-held towns. He not only told the Air Force where to bomb—but also and equally important to civilians, where not to bomb.

Tacloban is the capital of Leyte. A city of thirty thousand, it was understood to be heavily garrisoned by the Japanese. On the invasion plan this city was scheduled to be razed to the ground, for the beach immediately below would be the objective of a strong landing team.

On the eve of the bombings, with the planes literally warming up on the decks of the approaching carriers. Colonel Kangleon brought Chick word which sent the commander hurrying to his radio.

"Spare Tacloban," he pounded out frantically. "There are only civilians in the city."

Through their own sources the Japanese had become aware of the impending air raids. Tacloban was an obvious target. At the last moment, then, the Japanese had withdrawn all but a force of two hundred men from the capital and sealed the exits to civilians.

Let the Americans bomb Tacloban now, they thought. Let them kill innocent Filipinos while we shout, "Atrocity!" to the world.

"Those innocents," Colonel Kangleon added, "include my two children, my sister, and brother-in-law."

In mopping-up campaigns in southern Leyte, earlier in the war, the Japanese had captured these kinfolk of the guerrilla chieftain. Using them as hostages, they had threatened to kill them if Kangleon did not surrender.

Kangleon did not surrender.

To Chick's suggestion that they send in agents to endeavor to bring out his people, Kangleon turned a deaf ear.

"No, Commander," he said firmly. "I love my children and I'll pray to God every night that they may be spared. But I will not run the risk of retaliation against innocent people just to save my own."

"But we have no way of knowing whether or not my radio has reached the carriers in time to change the plan for Tacloban," Chick objected.

"So be it," said the colonel quietly. "My youngsters will simply have to take their chances with the rest."

Commander Parsons had not been wrong in recommending to Colonel Whitney and General MacArthur that Ruperto K. Kangleon be given the leadership in Leyte. Before everything else Kangleon was a patriot. His moral fiber was of steel. His troops faced a crucial baptism by fire. That the ordeal also held a personal agony for this Filipino father was unimportant to him.

"We are fighting a battle. Commander," he said simply.

Chick sent in word to the people of Tacloban to dig in as deeply as possible. As dawn of the sixteenth brought the hum of approaching B-24s he raised sleepless eyes toward the city. Chick knew how a father felt.

In came the bombers, blasting to shreds the beach defenses. The steel shovels of the explosives dug craters up to the very walls of the houses of Tacloban—and stopped. Not a bomb fell in the city proper during the four preliminary days before invasion.

There were still the Navy guns to consider. They may overshoot, Chick thought.

On D-Day the big guns of the fleet fingered the beach relentlessly for any pillboxes or gun positions that the bombers had missed. They did not touch the town however.

Not until the landing forces had freed Tacloban and restored Kangleon's children to his arms did Chick draw a free breath or know for sure that his warning had reached the fleet in time.

"You're a brave man, Colonel," he said in answer to Kangleon's expressions of gratitude. "I should hate to have had to make your decision. I doubt if I could have chosen as you did."

"I think you could," said the colonel.

In the invasion plan, Panaon Island and Panaon Strait were to be the objective of the veteran 4th Regimental Combat Team under the redoubtable Colonel Webber.

A terrific softening-up process was anticipated for this strategic region.

Immediately prior to the sixteenth. Chick had also learned that, while the Japanese had had a strong force on Panaon, this force had been removed at the last minute. In fact there were no Japs in the territory at all—but there were hundreds of civilians.

Panaon was farming country. The people had been going about their business with a minimum of interference from the Japanese. Everybody knew that Tacloban would be a target area, but why should anybody want to bomb a rural district with no Japanese around?

Chick answered this with a radio to his guerrilla agents on Panaon. "All parts of Leyte will be bombed," he told them, "and since the enemy has been in Panaon, it is logical to conclude that this island will be visited with destruction too. The people must be persuaded to go to the hills, take enough food for a week, and stay until the danger is over."

Chick's agents immediately reported that, while some of the more timid had taken this advice, the majority insisted in remaining in their towns and villages along the beaches. Would the commander, therefore, please do something?

Chick had foreseen this, and sent another desperate last-minute message out to the fleet. Just as in the case of Tacloban, the fleet—now underway— could not acknowledge this or any other message from Parsons. There was nothing to do but wait.

Small wonder that Commander Parsons got no sleep the night before the sixteenth of October.

Colonel Webber is an extremely rugged leader of a tough group of fighting men, selected to make beachheads in the most isolated spots and under the most difficult of conditions. Panaon, according to Army Intelligence, answered this description perfectly.

Yet the bombers passed it by and there was no preliminary naval barrage as the GIs went down the ropes. What was wrong? everybody wondered.

Armed to the teeth and doubly apprehensive because there had been no gun cover, Colonel Webber's Yanks charged ashore on Panaon—and stopped in their tracks. On the edge of the beach the entire populace was gathered as for fiesta. They were waving American flags. And the chorus that greeted the ears of the astonished infantrymen had nothing to do with the Banzai scream of the Japanese.

It was "God Bless America."

"Hell of a note," growled Colonel Webber later, to Chick Parsons, "when the toughest invasion force in the service has to go ashore at H-Hour without firing a shot—to join in a community sing."

In requesting that these two areas not be bombed. Chick had taken a long chance—as Colonel Whitney presently reminded him.

"We had to decide," said Whitney, "whether the Japs were playing a game in withdrawing from Tacloban before the bombing started. They might have returned after the barrage—and that would have been tragic for the American lads on the beach."

Chick had not taken this possibility into account, inasmuch as he knew that the Japanese did not expect a landing on Leyte. It was a sobering thought.

"However," he concludes, "the sparing of Tacloban caused much pleasure to General MacArthur and President Osmena when they came ashore on Dog Day. Maybe I stuck my neck out, but it was worth it to help the general bring deliverance and not death and destruction to the people. In other areas under fire all civilians were warned and no lives lost for lack of previous notice."

In order that Colonel Kangleon might most effectively co-ordinate the activities of his own forces with those of the various landing parties, Chick had been instructed to deliver the guerrilla chief to General Krueger as soon as possible on the morning of D-Day. He had likewise been ordered to present himself to Admiral Kinkaid's command ship to make report.

Wearying of waiting on the beach below Tacloban, Chick at length signaled a passing destroyer.

Quite naturally with D-Day less than twelve hours old, the flagship was much more interested in landing troops than in picking up one small party which had infiltrated ahead of time. The destroyer, contacting the admiral's ship, was simply instructed to pick up this party—with no explanation of its personnel or nature. It therefore put down a small boat full of armed men and precipitated a situation which Chick declared afterward "the most dangerous I have ever experienced."

"The beach," in Commander Parsons' own words, "was two miles from the nearest enemy and the men unable to understand why they should be sent ashore at this point.

"Through his glass the skipper of the small boat ascertained that most of our party of guerrillas was armed. This seemed to be proof enough for him that we were Japs and our signal a ruse to get aboard the destroyer.

"As they came nearer I could see that the sailors were prepared for a terrific battle. Every man wore a helmet and life jacket and carried a tommy gun. They were crouched down in the boat with only the top of their helmets and the muzzles of their weapons showing. The commanding officer had his pistol drawn. On both sides everybody was extremely nervous, for it must be remembered that this was D-Day.

"I knew that one shot from a jittery gob in the approaching boat would precipitate a volley from our guerrilla escort. None of these lads had ever seen an American warship in these waters before and all of them were perfectly willing to believe it might be a Jap vessel. In fact several of them warned me of this—which I knew, of course, couldn't be true—and asked me to be careful.

"To stay on the safe side, I decided to get in a small baroto with two un-armed Filipino boys and go out and meet the launch, which was now circling three hundred yards offshore, and showing definite signs of not wanting to come any farther. The situation did not seem to improve as I got closer.

"I have many more times been fired upon by friends than enemies and it looked as though I had gone through a lot of stuff only to have to take a bunch of lead from a gang of GI sailors sitting in a launch with their fingers trembling on the hair triggers of tommy guns.

"As soon as I got within hailing distance, I yelled, for Christ's sake come on in. Those things will hurt if they go off.'

"I could hear one of the Navy kids say, 'Gosh, Lieutenant, he speaks English. That guy ain't no Jap. Let's go in and see who he is.'

"At this there was a noticeable relaxation. The officer gave an audible sigh of relief and put his gun away in the holster. The men eased back in the boat and tension lifted on all sides. If I had been a Jap I don't know what I could have done—attacking a destroyer singlehanded—but the Nips have been known to try stupider things than that."

On the way to the command ship aboard the destroyer a Jap torpedo bomber flew in low and sent its missile against an American cruiser. Every ship in the fleet promptly turned loose with anti-aircraft fire. This was Commander Parsons' first intimate experience with naval fire of such magnitude and against a live target and made him yearn most fervently for the protection of his hills. Then and there Chick decided that if he took part in any more wars it would surely be as a jungle fighter and not in connection with any activity which required the pouring on or receiving of bombs, shells, and depth charges.

"Guerrilla life is hazardous," he said, "but nothing like this."

Aboard the command ship Colonel Kangleon was received by General Krueger and his staff with all the honor and respect due his position and ac-complishment among the guerrillas—in recognition of which General MacArthur shortly rewarded him with the Distinguished Service Cross and President Osmena with the governorship of Leyte.

Colonel Kangleon had brought with him his signal officer and his codes, and the guerrilla network was immediately setup in General Krueger's office and headquarters.

And this was Chick Parsons' day as well as Colonel Kangleon's. From the first to last he had every reason to say, "Leyte is a story of which I am very proud."

The day, however, was not yet over.

After making his report—and a few throwaway remarks—Chick borrowed the captain's tub for his first hot bath in ten days. He was enjoying the steamy water and the consciousness of a job well done when the operations officer appeared.

"We think it would be a good idea," the latter began, "for your guerrillas to clean up southern Leyte as you suggested just now."

Too late for inclusion in the strategy of D-Day, Commander Parsons had learned that southern Leyte was very lightly held by the Japanese. In fact from a line drawn across the province road from Baybay to Abuyog, the entire area to the south contained only two enemy garrisons.

In Malitbog forty or fifty Japanese soldiers had a small observation post. To the west, and also on the coast, Maasin was equally lightly held by a group whose chief function was to keep in touch with Jap forces on Cebu by radio. Both these towns had been visited by Chick on his first trip in to the Islands.

Chick had therefore suggested to the officers aboard ship that Malitbog and Maasin be given immediate attention to prevent the Japs from sending reinforcements over from Mindanao. In fact to point out how simple it would be, he had added: "The guerrillas could do it themselves if they had a couple of gunboats to knock down the walls of the garrisons."

From the tub Commander Parsons now endeavored to hedge. "I was merely trying to point out the simplicity of the operation with Colonel Webber's forces on Panaon in mind. They've got LCI gunboats and are looking for trouble. It's a natural—for Webber's men."

Webber, the operations officer replied, was busy holding the strait for the passage of PT boats and against any possible future Japanese attack. His team therefore could not be split up for such a project.

"You have indicated the ease with which it can be done to such a degree that General Krueger doesn't see any reason why the guerrillas don't drive out the Japs and liquidate those two garrisons. Since the gunboats are available, the general wants you to take over."

"Me?" Chick sat up. "I don't have any command function, either in the Army or the Navy."

"You do now, Commander."

Chick Parsons heaved himself out of the tub, wondering if he would ever learn to keep his trap shut and let well enough alone.

CHAPTER XVIII

MY POLICY OF NEVER ENGAGING THE JAPS IN OPEN combat went all to hell in a hand basket.

Early in the life of Spyron Commander Parsons had brought in to the guerrillas a number of splotched jungle suits, such as were commonly worn by American Marines in their first engagements in the Southwest Pacific. The guerrillas thought these outfits a great joke and gave them to their women to be made over into clothing for the children.

The guerrilla wanted no camouflage of cloth. He wanted something solid. Let him get behind a log, a tree, or an embankment, where he could pour a sudden volley of fire into a file of approaching Japanese and then melt away into the jungle, and he would give an excellent account of himself.

To proceed against a strongly fortified Jap position was something else. All Chick's previous effort had been directed toward dissuading the more hot-headed from such a course, which inevitably led to reprisals by the enemy against guerrilla and civilian alike. The danger of reprisals was lifted with the arrival of the Yanks. Yet ironically enough, Commander Parsons must now lead the guerrillas in just such a maneuver as he had formerly frowned upon.

Chick had the utmost faith in the little jungle fighters—in their element. He had often boasted of what they could do, given a little fire power, but he had not wanted to put this theory to the test. Not at this particular time, anyhow.

Nor was Chick deluded by the apparent casualness with which the general had given him this assignment. The eyes of the entire staff would be on the guerrillas. They would stand or fall on the success or failure of this mission, determining their future status in the retaking not only of Leyte but of the other islands.

Well before dawn of October 21 Commander Parsons flew to Sogod Bay, north of the town of Malitbog, to pick up a couple of LCI gunboats and contact the local guerrilla chief. Captain Juan Escano. His mind was full of misgivings which he confided freely to the young leader.

"I'm afraid I've got you lads way out on a limb," he apologized.

The captain waved this aside.

"Just knock a hole in the compound wall so we can get at the Japs. The guerrillas will do the rest," he said.

"I hope you're right. How many men can you roundup?"

"Two or three hundred."

Chick had hoped for a thousand. There was too much at stake, and he wished to leave no loophole for possible failure to slip through.

"Your men must be restrained until the barrage is over," he continued. "I think it best that you remain with them in the deployed area while I take over the raiding party. Are you familiar with the house and compound in which the Japanese are garrisoned?"

"I should be," said the captain. "It is the house of my grandfather."

"We'll probably have to knock the hell out of it."

Captain Escano shrugged.

"No matter," he said. "It can be rebuilt."

The compound and house stood right on the beach of the town. The residence was two stories high with a patio in the Spanish style. Within the compound was an intricate system of trenches and roofed dugouts. About the whole enclosure ran a stout adobe-stone fence, ten feet high, thirty inches thick—impregnable to ordinary rifle fire or assault.

This would be the immediate objective of shellfire.

Commander Parsons spent the night aboard ship and before dawn had the two gunboats about a mile offshore and beyond range of anything the garrison might offer in the way of firepower. In the darkness the guerrilla leader had deployed his men in depth about the garrison, surrounding every possible avenue of retreat, but out of range of fire from the LCIs.

The moment was at hand. There was no grin on Chick's face as he addressed the waiting gunners.

"I want you boys to remember that we're endeavoring to bring liberation, and not death and destruction, to this town and its people," he said. "It has not been possible to evacuate all the civilian populace. The church and other buildings are very close to the Jap compound. Be careful and not overshoot the target."

The gunners nodded. They knew their business.

Chick looked at his watch. It was five-fifteen.

"Commence firing," he ordered.

The first shells promptly announced the new partnership between the United States Navy and the guerrilla-soldiers of the Philippines.

With each crashing salvo the gunboats crept a few hundred yards nearer shore. Due to the shelving nature of the beach, the last round roared in at point-blank range of not over one hundred yards.

Chick gave the signal to cease firing and studied the target with his field glasses. The compound wall was breached in several places. The residence itself exhibited signs of considerable damage. Outside of a brief spray of machine-gun bullets, fired wildly from an upper window in answer to the first shells, there had been no reply from the enemy.

Leaving one gunboat standing guard offshore, Chick moved the other up the beach about a quarter of a mile. Here, beneath an American flag, a raiding party of fifty guerrillas waited. Scattered rifle shots could be heard from the rest of the force ambushed about the garrison and the fingers of the little brown raiders itched with impatience.

"Hurry, Commander," said one of the eager youngsters. "Otherwise we miss all the fun."

Chick grinned.

"Let's go," he said, and they started off on the double. Slipping through the silent town, Chick and the guerrillas crept through breaches in the compound wall. The party was divided and while one group poked into the trenches and dugouts the other, under Chick's leadership, rushed the house. For the first time Chick was carrying a gun—borrowed from one of the guerrillas.

Without opposition they entered and started systematic search. In the basement was stored tons of food, clothing, and ammunition—but no Japanese. His automatic ready, Chick mounted to the second floor, where he found complete denial of the theory that the Japanese prefer death to flight.

In the galley on the upper deck rice still bubbled on the stove, dishes were still hot. The beds showed signs of recent occupancy and even more recent abandonment. Mosquito nets hung in shreds and everything pointed to a frantic, disorganized departure. Here and there pools of blood gave evidence that the shells had found human marks, but the building was otherwise completely empty.

The enemy had not gotten far, however. Captain Escano's men had cut down the entire garrison force as they came over the wall. Not a man escaped.

"Any prisoners?" Chick inquired when he received this report.

"We took three from the dugouts."

"Good. See that they aren't harmed. Did we suffer any casualties?"

"No sir."

The gunboat shells had so terrified the Japanese that their only thought had been to get away to the hills. Many of them had thrown away their guns in flight. The victory was complete.

Poking about among the rooms. Chick found three radios in good working order.

He dispatched a message to COM 7th Fleet:

Maasin mission successful, town returned to grateful populace, proceeding to second objective.
Parsons

Runners had already gone to the hills to inform the inhabitants that the town was free. A happy procession began to stream back in, bundles of much-transported possessions on their heads. Leading the balikuate came the familiar figure of Chick's old friend, the mayor.

"Commander Parsons," he cried in joy and recognition. "Once again you have brought us glad tidings."

"The town is yours, Mayor," said Chick, shaking his hand. "For good, this time."

"The Japanese will not return?"

"I doubt it. The Americans are still landing by the thousands. The Japanese have their hands full farther north. Rest easy—and get that dock fixed, hey?"

The mayor laughed.

"Ah, you have not forgotten my sudden descent through the pier on the occasion of your other visit?"

"Not likely." Chick grinned.

"And we shall never forget you, Commander. Malitbogand its people are eternally yours."

The jubilant populace pressed around Commander Parsons, trying in every way possible to show their gratitude. Even the old gentleman whose house had been ruined by the shells grasped his hand, tears in his eyes.

"What is a house," he said, to Chick's apologies, "compared to the slaying of the dragon?"

"Now," said the old mayor, "we shall really hold a fiesta. You will be our guest of honor, Commander Parsons."

But Chick's job was only half done. With difficulty he extricated himself from the embraces of the people and turned toward Maasin.

The objective in the case of this second town consisted of a school building of imposing size with some lesser structures, the whole set in a much greater space of ground than at Malitbog. There was no compound wall to contend with, but the entire area was fenced in by bristling barbed-wire entanglements.

Within the garrison were lodged some fifty or sixty Japanese whose primary purpose was radio observation, but who might be expected to possess considerable arms and ammunition, as well as sufficient supplies to withstand a long siege—unless they could be knocked out by the gunboats.

Maasin also differed in another respect with which the guerrilla leader immediately acquainted Chick as they jogged toward town in a two-wheeled carromata drawn by a small pony.

"Two of our agents have access to the garrison," said the guerrilla leader.

Free to come and go at will were an old washerwoman and the mayor, who posed as a puppet and headed the Japanese constabulary in the town but who actually was working very closely with the guerrillas.

"Good," said Chick. "If these friends can give us the plan of the interior we shall be able to direct our fire against individual objectives."

Without warning, at this point, a rifle cracked sharply. A little spurt of dust lifted from the road just ahead of the pony.

"Snipers," cried the guerrilla chief, and wheeled the carromata with a quick twist of his wrists, almost throwing Chick out of the cart. With bullets singing around them, they dashed back down the road to a turn and safety.

"Sorry, Commander," said the chief. "I had become so interested in what you propose to do that I had forgotten there are snipers operating in this area."

Chick mopped his brow. "I take it your boys have been bothering the Nips a bit."

"We have done what we could. With the assistance of your gunboats, we ought to be able to finish the job. You wish to interview His Honor?"

"As soon as possible."

The mayor was brought to headquarters.

"Hola! It is I, Commander," said the mayor with a wide grin.

"We know that you have had access to the Japanese garrison. I want you to give me the detailed setup and especially the spots where we can do the most harm in the quickest time."

The loyal Filipino official proceeded to give Commander Parsons the most detailed information as to the disposition of the Japs in the schoolhouse, the location of their guns, and even the battle stations of each person.

"Great stuff," Chick applauded. "The gunners will love this."

The mayor looked sad.

"It is necessary, I suppose, to destroy our school?"

"I'm afraid so," said Chick, and hesitated. "Unless the Japs can be per-suaded to surrender."

"They might," said the mayor, "if they realize they are facing naval guns as well as guerrilla troops."

"Let's send in a note by the washerwoman and see what happens," said Chick, and quickly drew up a demand for the Japanese to surrender, pointing out that they were hopelessly outnumbered and that resistance was useless.

The lavandera trundled off and shortly reappeared with an answer from the Jap sergeant in command.

"Reinforcements are expected momentarily from Cebu," was the gist of this defy. "The Japanese never surrender. We shall fight to the last man."

Chick immediately regretted his note, which had only served to alert the enemy.

"They're probably buzzing Cebu by radio right now," he said. "We'll have to work fast."

This situation caused Commander Parsons to spend another sleepless night. Maasin was well away from Leyte Gulf and protecting air control. Cebu was very close and even closer were Japanese forces on Bohol. Jap PT boats were based in Cebu and it was not beyond imagination that they might send over a raiding party in these swift craft.

Chick therefore ordered a couple of PT boats, to forestall this possibility, and nervously waited for the dawn, sure that something would happen.

And something did.

With the first light of day a Japanese lugger was observed beached below the garrison. Chick leveled his glasses and found no evidence of personnel aboard the 180-foot craft. The lugger had apparently come over with supplies during the night.

"We could use that vessel," said the guerrilla chief.

Chick nodded and spoke to the gunners.

"Put a couple of .50-caliber shells into her superstructure," he ordered.

The gunners did as directed. Instantly four Japanese darted out of the lugger and sprinted up the beach.

"They won't get far with that," Chick murmured, for guerrilla forces were already hidden about the garrison.

A burst of rifle fire stretched the four Japs in the sand. This proved the signal for launching the bombardment, as return fire came from Jap machine guns in the pillboxes surrounding the garrison.

"Knock off those pillboxes, boys," Chick shouted.

The gunners depressed their weapons and quickly silenced opposition from the pillboxes. Then they tore great holes in the barbed-wire barricade.

A few Japanese scurried from their trenches and futilely tried to make their way to safety. But the majority remained in the schoolhouse.

Like the garrison building at Malitbog, this structure had a galvanized iron roof and the first story was composed of adobe and stone. But unlike it, the Maasin schoolhouse was of wood in its upper portion, and there were wooden frames in the windows throughout.

"Load the .20-caliber cannon with incendiaries," Chick now ordered the gunners. "Direct fire against the upper portion of the building."

In a matter of minutes the top story of the schoolhouse was a roaring inferno. In a panic the Japanese began to stream from the burning structure. This proved too much for guerrilla discipline. Before Chick could reach shore, the raiding party dashed in with spitting carbines and hand grenades to finish off the enemy. Bolos rose and fell in the early morning sun as the guerrillas made sure their fallen adversaries stayed down for good.

Uttering wild battle cries, the guerrillas then charged the building proper.

The remaining Jap defenders, seeing that their situation was hopeless, with flame at their back and fury approaching, exposed themselves in windows and doorways. They pulled the pins on grenades and held them to their chests.

"Banzai!" they shouted, even as they disintegrated.

By the time Chick could reach the main building the place was a shambles. Such Japanese inside as did not commit suicide were roasted alive. The sound of combat echoed and died until there was nothing but the roaring of the flames, completing the job the gunboats and guerrillas had begun.

No prisoners were taken.

Chick sent another radio to COM 7th Fleet. Southern Leyte was again free. The guerrillas had met the test."

For which thank heaven," Chick added fervently.

Colonel Kangleon had wished to accompany Commander Parsons on the move against these Jap garrisons. This was impossible as he was needed to direct the action of his troops along the escape routes farther north. However, he had followed Chick's progress with the most breathless interest and on his return gave Commander Parsons a hero's welcome.

"Congratulations on your successful termination of these engagements," he said.

"I'd hardly call them that. Colonel," said Chick. "They were only forays, at best."

Both of them knew the significance of this action, however.

"When word came in that Malitbog had fallen," said Colonel Kangleon, "the Sixth Army staff was delighted. Now, with Maasin, you have proved beyond any possibility of doubt just what the guerrilla-soldiers can do, aided by firepower. General Krueger is tremendously pleased and impressed, and so am I."

"Thank you, Colonel. Your boys deserve all the credit. They could have done the same thing as the Navy, given their own artillery and land-based mortars."

"They will have that opportunity soon, thanks to you. Chick. The Army has promised this type of equipment."

All over the southern and central islands, wherever American bombs fell and American troops moved, guerrilla-soldiers moved with them. On Leyte, Mindanao, Samar, Spyron rifles and carbines and tommy guns mowed down the enemy. Everywhere the fleeing Japs were caught between a fiery vise welded by free Americans, free Filipinos. And presently Chick could confide to Colonel Whitney:

"It looks to me as though Spyron's job is done."

"And Parsons'?" inquired the colonel.

Chick sat down, suddenly very weary. He had been on the dead dig for many days, sleeping and eating little, fighting to keep going and discharge his many heavy responsibilities. Reaction was setting in with a vengeance.

"Why don't you go home and see your folks and take care of that malaria. Chick?" the colonel inquired anxiously.

"Do you suppose they'd let me go?" Chick inquired innocently. "I had a leave less than two years ago."

The colonel smiled.

"I think they would," he said gently. "After all, it's been quite a two years, hasn't it?"

EPILOGUE

Regarding my present activities . . .

Comdr. C. Parsons, USNR
Com 7th Fleet, Staff (3)
Fleet Post Office,
San Francisco, Cal. 1 April 1945.

Dear Trav:

After a brief hospitalization for malaria in Asheville, North Carolina, I returned to the Philippines in January 1945. Without caring to use the vertical pronoun, I found on my return that I was supposed to double and treble my efforts at supplying the guerrillas so as to increase their usefulness and thereby lessen the effort subsequently to be needed by the Yanks to knock out the enemy in the various by-passed areas.

A personal trip to each area and a long talk with my old friends, the district commanders, brought about a good understanding of the true situation and therefore happiness all around.

By plane and small surface craft I have made frequent trips back to guerrilla country and have had a go at an enemy installation—report received after the action says three hundred killed. I have also worked out with the guerrillas a network of airfields, some of them quite close to enemy concentrations, which will handle C-47 transport plane shipments. Now we can get to the various areas in a hurry and do in hours what it took me months to do by sub.

When the internment camp at Manila was released I found an excuse to make a trip or so up there by plane and my portable para-bike, and found that Katsy's mother had been taken from Welfareville with four other women just before the invasion of Manila. She was not at Santiago or Mantinglupa. There is a faint chance that she may be at Baguio, which is still heavily held—but I am afraid she has paid heavily for being my mother-in-law. So far Tommy Jurika, her son who is on duty here with me—and I have both drawn a blank.

Manila is finished, completely demolished. I have seen sights that I shall remember a long time. I arrived on the heels of the Yanks as they pushed the enemy down the Boulevard toward the Luneta, and visited the house of a good friend, Don Carlos Perez Rubio, a wealthy Spanish-Filipino. In the garden of the house I counted twenty-two bodies—the entire family including

women and children, three people who were visiting at the time, and servants—liquidated in a most brutal fashion. Bayonets mostly. A number of my
other old friends have suffered a like fate.

Such sights give me a feeling of satisfaction at having been in a small
part connected with the elimination of a few Nips here and there. I could
never feel conscience-stricken after viewing some of the results of Jap atrocities in Manila.

The guerrillas have been spurred to greater deeds with the stepped-up
arrival of supplies by plane and by my little LCI fleet. Added to which has
been close co-ordination with air support to hit specific targets and enemy
concentrations. In short the guerrillas definitely have the Jap on the run and
will make further invasions by American troops (if and when) much simpler—
thus saving a lot of American lives. This is probably the best dividend which
will be realized from Uncle Doug's investment in support of the guerrilla
movement.

The guerrillas are grand people and I will never let them down so long as
they need me. In living with them for two years and knowing their key men
by first name, there has never been any doubt in my mind as to what they
could do. People who do not know the guerrillas are sometimes reluctant to
share this belief. That is because the guerrilla has not been built up as a grand
soldier.

In a GI sense I do not think he is a grand soldier. He is a jungle fighter,
pure and simple, and would not be particularly effective in an infantry company fighting open warfare. He is a specialist in his own line and as a guerrilla
he is, in my opinion, the best in the world.

The importance of the guerrilla-soldier will not cease with the end of this
war. These men who have been out in the hills fighting and harassing the Japs
naturally feel they have a right to be heard in the government and future of
the Philippine Islands. They are not interested in independence from the
United States at this time and any leader who attempts to govern without
taking the guerrillas into consideration will be making a sad mistake.

What the future will be it is of course impossible to say. The present is still
too much with us and we just plug along from day to day.

Regarding my present activities, they are not at all interesting.

Mabuhay, Reed.
(Signed) Chick

Made in the USA
Monee, IL
04 June 2020